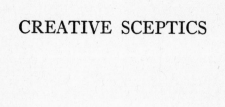

CREATIVE SCEPTICS

CREATIVE SCEPTICS

In defense of the liberal temper

By T. V. SMITH

Professor of Philosophy
The University of Chicago

WILLETT, CLARK & COMPANY

CHICAGO   NEW YORK

1934

PREFACE

The day of tired liberals is passing, passing in many places through the ' liquidation ' of liberalism itself. Lusty radicals now strut and fret their hour upon the world's stage, doubling all too often for confident reactionaries who take their ease behind the scenes. Who knows but that historic fact may connive with humane hope that their play be brief? Never doubt that, soon or late, the glitter of radicalism will also pass and the ease of reactionaries behind the scenes turn to nervousness as mutterings mount in the darkening audience. No curtain calls in the pageantry of time for such as turn their backs on men and shudder at the face of fate.

When the curtains have fallen and night has overtaken all who use opportunity ill, will not it then be day for the temperate, the wise, the good?

But who are the temperate, the wise, the good? — who but you, and you, and you, my readers — all! Who of you does not volunteer for the honor of such fair-seeming sounds? I wish to volunteer myself. But that makes too many of us; for who's left to be the ' tired liberal,' the ' lusty radical,' the ' confident reactionary '? Do I hear volunteers for these dour epithets? I hear none — there seems to be none — there is none.

This is a most embarrassing discovery, is it not? The sheep and the goats are mingling with each other, right along, and no shepherd's crook, though no dearth of would-be shepherds, to separate them. Why you yourself, my gentlest reader, may not be a sheep after all. I myself might be a goat. This is for a fact embarrassing.

I have written a book here, for you, that may throw some light upon our predicament. I hope so; for otherwise there remains only the fun of writing it. That was great. But my fun can only be fulfilled if you find here some way to tell whether you are a sheep or I am a goat.

April 2, 1934,
Birthday of Thomas Jefferson   T. V. S.

CONTENTS

vii

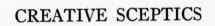

CREATIVE SCEPTICS

CHAPTER I

THE ONSET AND UPSET OF SCEPTICISM

Being an earnest soliloquy with the reader

Come now, hopeful reader, and please be good enough at once to put yourself back into that literary forest of your childhood. Let it be, if you list, a forest primeval, and you be there quite alone. Listen, pray, with the mind's ear to that falling tree. Tell me truly now, would there have been any sound had your ear not been there to hear that mighty tree come crashing down? Would there?

Just as I had feared — you are now too old to be caught, and too wise longer to be amused by the question. Being sophisticated, you well know that there would be no sound; for, as I hear you trying to tell me through this print that separates us, you are well aware that ' sound ' is what is heard. No ear, then, no sound. Vibrations, of course, there would be, and they would beat against other trees. But vibrations must beat against an ear-drum and throb their way through it into the brain before sound is born. Now that you have that out of your way, you feel mildly proud of yourself, don't you? How splendid it is to be grown at last, and to know things.

3

I. Weaving the Web of Doubt

But stay! You are not going to get away so easily. I am a philosopher, doomed to puzzle others, as Socrates said of himself and all our breed, because I myself am puzzled. Look back at what you have admitted. Consider whether you have anything to retract — and consider it well. For I am about to tell you that on that little matter of sound you have said something that will bother you to your dying day. You see nothing wrong with what you have admitted in that second paragraph? Then are you damned; for, on the mellowed maxim that he who doubts is damned already, I am going to plunge you into a river of doubt from which better men than you — and women, too, though by your winsome smiles out there, some of you seem to say no! — better ones than you, I surmise, have struggled all their lives to be free — vainly struggled.

> For once in the river of ruin,
> What boots it, to do or to dare,
> For down we must go
> In the turbulent flow,
> To the desolate sea of Despair.

You may quit me as your guide, but you will not be quit of me, unless you quit me here and now; for from here on I am gently whispering into your ear this troublesome thing: that by your being so certain that there can be no sound without an ear, you are never going to be as certain again of many things much more important. I warn you that looking longingly back upon this day's — or is it night's? — work, you will many a time henceforth feel again with my poet — Paul Laurence Dunbar — that

> Long time ago, we two set out,
>> My soul and I.
>> I know not why,
> For all our way was dim with doubt.
>> I know not where
>> We two may fare;
> Though still with every changing weather,
> We wander, groping on together.

I make bold, helpless reader, to say all this, and even to quote poetry about it, because if sound requires an ear, then sight requires an eye; then taste requires a tongue; then smell requires a nose; then weight requires a muscle; then touch requires a skin. Now in all earnestness tell me what is left of this book you are reading: after its shape, color, weight, meaning if any, and mayhap smell are all sucked up into the mind. That book right there in your hand, I mean — the one I've written for you! Open your mouth and tell me what is left of it. ' But,' I think I hear you hedging, ' the real book is not in my mind at all; it's still out there in my hand.' So I heard you say. Very well, tell me about it; even write me a letter about it if you think you can do a better job that way (only after

5

you've read it all, however!). Just tell me what that ' real ' book, as you call it, the one out there in your hands, pray tell me what it is. I dare you to open your mouth, or put a pen to paper without calling out one of these qualities I've mentioned, or another like them, if I've forgotten to mention all of them. And every single one of them by the admission you've made about sound, is put right on the brain, or if you prefer, inside the mind.

The simple truth seems to be that you are holding out there in your hands a bundle of mental qualities, if you are holding anything. Or are you now inclined to turn upon me, its author, with the admission that in holding my book, you are literally holding nothing at all, just nothing? Even so, you're caught; go so far as to call the book ' rotten '; you are not going thereby to get full relief. I've hit you, I can see that; but your wound is inside, it is deep — and what are you going to do about it? Even if you were close enough to throw the book at me, you'd feel no better afterwards in the spot where I've hit you than Dr. Johnson felt after bruising his ponderous foot against the stone in order to refute Philosopher Berkeley, who first made this matter grievously clear to his generation.

I'm no Bishop Berkeley (though I'm to tell you of him at the end of the next chapter), but I'm determined that you too are going to get this matter clear, despite my knowledge that it's going to make you quite unhappy if you really do get it clear. I

6

insist upon your getting it clear, even at the cost of your poise and pain, because if you do not get it clear, you're going right on making other people miserable as long as you live. In a world where so much misery is inflicted, it ought in all conscience to be passed around. The surest way to pass it around is to begin at home, to force people who are primed to perpetrate injury, to inflict part of it upon themselves rather than all of it upon others. If offense must come, as our Great Teacher said, then let at least some of it *come* — rather than make all of it *go*. Even if my teaching you how to bedevil yourself does not stop you from inflicting misery upon others, it will unquestionably let you know how it feels.

You see already what I mean. Or do you? It is this: much of the misery that men inflict upon one another is in the name of and because of their feeling so certain that they know things and that the other fellow does not. Now a person who must suffer you to thrust upon him your notions of right and wrong, good and bad, truth and falsity is doubly wronged. He's not only run over, dominated by you, as it were; but he's in the same act denied the positive privilege of withholding acquiescence until, convinced, he gives full consent. To treat a fellow man so is to add to clear insult definite injury. Intolerance is man's worst inhumanity to man. Some men may dominate others now and then out of sheer cruelty, but not many nor for long.

7

Most men dominate because they're just so right that they spill over the hot stuff of their inner convictions and are glad to see it burn its way down the other fellow's throat. There is quite probably no way of getting men to quit inflicting this double wrong upon their fellows except to shake their confidence in their own infallibility. No man is too shrinking to be pope to himself, infallible when speaking universally upon faith and morals. ' Persecution for the expression of opinion,' as Justice Holmes so searchingly says, ' seems perfectly logical. If you have no doubt of your premises or of your power and want a certain result with all your heart you . . . naturally sweep away all opposition.'

That is just what I've been trying to tell you, foolish reader. It takes a wise man like the great Justice to tell it to you properly, and I'm going to give him a freer chance at you later on. But right from the beginning I'm going to press you — though I'll ram no beliefs down your throat — until you admit that you're no wiser than the rest of us.

To get you to doubt yourself is, or may be, a first step toward confidence in your fellows, or, if not confidence, then at least sympathy for the rest of us. And to acquire this virtue would be worth while if it took you all night and left you weary in the cold grey dawn. In teaching you the penance of doubt, I've begun as you see at the very bottom.

I'm not concerned with the parochial trivialities of teaching you to question the Constitution or wonder about the existence of God; it's the world itself and all that fills it out there which you're in danger of losing. Your grand beliefs may be allowed to take care of themselves in the event; but I will take no chance on your longer fooling yourself as to the certainty of your humblest knowledge. You have already admitted — don't forget that — that there is no sound without an ear.

Admitting that, you can claim to know precious little for certain. You're already a sceptic, to tell you the brutal truth; and if it's the first time you've seen yourself as others constantly see you — in the guise of a braggart out-talking his information — it's not going to be the last time, however little you enjoy it. While I've got you caught and, I hope, in a somewhat contrite mood, I'm going to ask you to see the thing through, going to pledge you not to jump in the lake or off a skyscraper until you see how much company you have. In loving company your misery may at last commiserate itself. I want to show you the depths of scepticism into which you are already sinking, its varieties, its penalties, and at last some of the tempered hopes and chastened beliefs that have been born of its discipline. I do not promise you salve for all wounds, pay enough for all the pains; but I'll show you how out of doubt Descartes found himself, how Spinoza found peace, how Berkeley found God, how Hume

9

found courage to be honest, Schopenhauer sympathy, Montague courage for the ills of life and enthusiasm for its goods, and how Holmes doubted his way to Democracy. You may not find all these virtues for yourself. But some of these sceptics will discover to you at least something in what will at times appear perhaps a seamless web of despair. If I, weaving in and out of the webs woven by these wise men, can make a democrat of you — making you first humble, then proud, and at last tolerant — I shall let you count as pure velvet whatever else you receive from scepticism. Before I turn, however, to draw my morals from modern sceptics, let me tell you, quite briefly, of a certain brand of ancient scepticism. It will furnish us a background for our major task.

II. On Doubting Whether We Doubt

The brand of scepticism that prevailed among some of the ancients has become legendary. It has less to teach us than has modern doubt; and so we shall not tarry long with it. It had without a doubt an element of showmanship in it, and better illustrates the neutral, not to say negative, side of doubt. We shall not hesitate to point out its ground, or its merit; but we shall pass as quickly as may be from it to later times to see what men more like us have suffered, learned, and taught from the depths of doubt.

It was Pyrrho of the second century before our era whom fact or fancy has crowned king of historic sceptics. From him primarily sprang the jibes we read in our school books of men who did not know what or whether they knew, who doubted whether they doubted. Now Pyrrho was, for a fact, quite a doubter. He not only doubted this and that, but he gave many reasons why what men call knowledge is not and cannot be knowledge. What is more he even gave his theory the final seal of practice and refused to trust so-called truth more than doubt. On a walk, it is said, he would approach a precipice. Or was it a precipice? His companions so identified it, and his own eyes reported the same. But Pyrrho, trusting nothing more than anything else, would walk right off the precipice — did his friends not pull him back.

Friends are good companions on paths where there are precipices. One hesitates to think what would have been the effect if he had been at the wheel of a Packard. The machine age has disciplined our doubts as well as dampened our hopes. Nor were wagons or dogs anything to Pyrrho, so it is said; for he did not trust his senses at all. He'd beard a bulldog as quickly as a toy monkey and run over a wagon at the drop of a hat — did his friends not stop him. His disciples accompanied him wherever he went. One can almost hear Pyrrho breathing aloud the Socratic tribute to friendship: ' I have a passion for friends; and I would rather have a good friend than the best cock or quail in the world: I would even go further, and say the best horse or dog. Yea, by the dog of Egypt, I should greatly prefer a real friend to all the gold of Darius, or even to Darius himself: I am such a lover of friends as that.'

Pyrrho had indeed much cause to love his friends; he lived to the ripe old age of ninety years, it is said; and died at last, I believe, in bed. You might like, in a curious moment, to turn back and scan his maxims. In a veritable decalogue of doubt, he summarizes in ' ten modes of argument ' the human quest for knowledge, every one of which spells scepticism at the end. You will find them in the *Life of Pyrrho*, by Diogenes Laertius, (conveniently quoted in my book *Philosophers Speak for Themselves*).

Showmanship apart, this type of scepticism clearly served some defensive rôle in the age in which it flourished. In that sense it, too, was constructive, though not as creative as modern doubt. It flourished indeed at a time when most sensitive men needed defenses against the course of external events, and so it tinged all ancient schools of thought for several centuries. (E. Zeller tells this story in great detail in his book, *Stoics, Epicureans and Sceptics*.) The world had gone wrong. The Epicureans with a philosophy whose joy of life others have envied, even while reproaching it, gathered themselves together in small groups in order to shut the world out. They were in their own eyes, as was another group of which St. Paul tells us, ' men of whom the world was not worthy.' ' Friend,' as the legend ran over the Garden of Epicurus, ' here it will be well for you to abide; here pleasure is the highest good. . . . These gardens do not provoke hunger, but quench it; they do not cause a greater thirst by the very drinks they afford, but assuage it by a remedy which is natural and costs nothing.' Bread and water in peace are sometimes more to be desired than much more at the price of din. Rationality may preserve itself on humble means in a world run amuck.

Stoicism made a general virtue of the indifference which the Epicureans embraced as a specific defense. The Sage became the man who could appear the same no matter what. It is not merely the world that is the soul's enemy. Its dearest enemies are of its own household. Man's emotions are not subject to reason. They war with reason. Reason, however, may be master in a house without being master of it. Pathos is the price of pride, but pride can preserve the soul's purity. One may discern the pride through the rents, as the wit remarked to Diogenes; but patches need not destroy even if they reveal pride. The wise man grows in untoward times to be he whose pride in reason is inexorable. To him the world is only what he allows it to be. To keep outer recalcitrance made to order, however, the Stoic had sometimes greatly to narrow the apertures.

It was this narrowing process which the sceptics continued until no crack was left. The Epicureans narrowed pleasures to the thinner intellectual ones and social intercourse to the affinity of kindred groups. The Stoics narrowed life down to no pleasures save the austere fruits of pride. The soul was shut up in a prison house so grey that it ceased to be a vice, even appears at times to have been esteemed a virtue, ' to open the door ' and let the soul go free. In this protective prison house the sceptics, as I have said, left no crack unguarded. No, not even the crack of truth, through which, alas, many an error has skipped in. He who will not choose cannot suffer the pains of wrong choice. He who will not make up his mind at all cannot fall into error. This was indeed mind's final defense against life — against even its own life.

Now, without much doubt, all this austere heroism of the ancients demands its meed of praise. Not the less so because it did not in any of the schools always maintain itself at white heat. Lapses from heroism may be pathetic, but they are never puerile. Let us not, therefore, withdraw one iota of fame that legend has woven around the heads of these heroes of doubt — least of all from the head of Pyrrho. Even so, it is not such scepticism as this that is most creative and so with which we are here primarily concerned. We ourselves do not seek to build defenses against life, but surely also not to dispraise those who have found it necessary to do so. We seek, rather, to know the worst in order to make out of it the very best we can.

III. RETURNING TO THE WEB WEAVING

It may be that through all these preliminaries you have been smiling to yourself while scowling at me. I see through your scowling smile certain comforts you have slyly reserved for yourself. You are thinking, for instance, that this ancient scepticism was a game, which since you do not elect to play, you need not suffer the penalties. We shall see what comfort there is in that thought when we face the same technique where it is not a game, in modern life and thinkers. But are you thinking also that the illustration which I chose at the beginning leaves you a loophole? I chose sight as the sense with which to embarrass you. 'Seeing,' perhaps you are saying to yourself, 'is not the only way to believing; feeling is much closer to knowledge than is seeing.' 'That,' you may say, 'is as clear as the nose on your face.'

Take your nose, since you mention it. How much do you know about it? Well, you know that you can blow it, of course. But the blowing is sound, as you see; and we have already disposed of sound, tucking it safely away in the mind. If you are feminine, you can powder the nose. But you can do that much more evenly if you are looking through the mirror at what you are doing. Still, I grant you that there is feeling in both the blowing and the powdering. Take what comfort you can from that for the moment, for I am going on to ask you, in the rhyme of Friedrich Schiller —

> Many a year I've used my nose
> To smell the onion and the rose;
> Is there any *proof* which shows
> That I've a right to that same nose?

Nor am I content merely to ask you that; I am going to answer it. The answer is no. That nose on your face, than which normally nothing could be plainer, is not as plain as you could wish. If you know it there by sound, that's out; by sight, that's out. But of course there does remain ' feeling.' Now feeling may mean ' touch ' or it may mean something very much more vague. The vague meaning is also out, for though in our inner private life we depend a great deal upon what we ' feel,' none of us claims very much for it as a way of settling doubt regarding outer things. It raises more doubt than it settles, when so used. I think that you will be uneasy enough about relying upon that sort of ambiguity without my pressing you upon the point. So I shall pass it here, though I do not mean to forget it for good.

'Touch' as a tangible form of feeling, however, does remain as your last sensory resort to prove that your nose is still out there on your face instead of now safely within your mind. You have two forms of touch, in fact, to depend upon. The first is the touch of the particles that you smell, upon the sensitive lining of the nose. Though neither you nor I usually think of this, it is true that before we can smell, we must actually have things up our noses, which means actually against our inner noses. Though a distance-sense, the nose is also this contact-sense. So deft is the contact, however, that we ordinarily say that we smell, rather than feel, the particles that visit us from more or less distant bodies. We would not 'smell' them, however, unless we first 'felt' them. 'All smells,' observes Plato, 'are thinner than water and thicker than air.'

Now when we've got it down to that fine point, I think you'll agree that I do not need to argue the matter. We shall not in this book resort to plain hard proof where we can proceed by consent. You agree — do you not? — that smells are not to be considered as objective as are sights and sounds? Then we agree to let the smelling aspect of your nose slide back into your mind. You are quite right, however, in holding on to the outer nose, the one which you touch with your fingers.

If we slip here, no sense is left.

Ah, but this be a venturesome journey,
Forever those things are ashift,
And a step to one side
Means a grasp of the tide,
And the current is fearful and swift.

So much indeed depends here upon not slipping, or letting slip, that I'll pardon you if you insist upon holding your nose the remainder of this séance. Then, you'll have the satisfaction of knowing that if your whole nose slips back into the mind, your fingers are gone also. Now, what reason is there for thinking that touch deserves the credence we put in it as our last proof of an external nose — and world? Precious little indeed, save that men do trust it more than any other sense. But we cannot allege even general trust when it is trust that is being called in question.

If we turn to psychology to tell us about the senses, it tells us a story regarding touch no different from the stories of the senses we have already noted. And that story is that the sense-organs are known in no other way than are other things, that is, by sense-qualities. In smelling things, we infer the nose as the organ just as we infer the presence of the thing smelt. But it is qualities, whatever sense-organ they come through, which we actually know. Touch is just as much a quality as is sound, sight, or odor. For all the contact, touch gets the object no nearer the mind than does any other sense, until it gets it *in* the mind — and that's too late to save the nose on our faces. To argue the matter out to a demonstration of the nerve-endings in the skin and the way they transmit what at the threshold of the mind is transmuted into sensations or ideas, would make the matter no clearer; for it is clear at the beginning as at the end of such demonstration that what we feel is ' feeling,' not the objects which we say ' cause ' the feelings. The person who hopes to shortcircuit doubt by appealing to touch is touching he knows not what, he knows not where.

Neither the philosophers nor the psychologists are inclined to trust to touch more than to other senses in order to prove indubitable knowledge of external objects, not even of the nose on your face. This fact, especially with reference to the philosophers, will become gradually apparent through later chapters, and with it the force of the argument here only sketched against unqualified trust of any or all the senses as adequate antidotes to doubt. We cannot forbear quoting in this place, however prematurely, the pathetic conclusion reached by one American philosopher who has worried much over this whole matter. ' We are confined,' confesses Roy Wood Sellars, in his *Evolutionary Naturalism,* ' to the subjective side and can never have in consciousness the existent known, though we can literally grasp it with our hands.' To add to the natural pathos here the pathos of criticism, we have only to recall that ' our hands ' are no longer there to do the grasping; for with the first clause of Sellars' sentence the hands have either themselves slipped into consciousness or they are forever beyond the reach of knowledge. Seeing it so, I need not now request you to free your nose from the desperate clutch you have all this while had upon it in order to reassure yourself; for now both nose and fingers have yielded their external substance to the tenuous qualities of mind, or they are for good and all beyond the reach of mind.

IV. The Fearful Price of Certain Knowledge — Solipsism

Still, that last clause embodies a large conclusion, ' for good and all beyond the reach of mind.' ' Are you not using the term mind,' you ask me, ' to mean more than any or all the senses? ' You are right; and perhaps we ought, therefore, to ask whether the mind, being more than the senses, does not have power to know without the senses, to reach beyond them? We need something more, now that you've let yourself be maneuvered into the position of one of Cowper's character's —

> He would not, with a peremptory tone,
> Assert the nose upon his face his own.

That the mind can truly know what the senses bring it, we have not yet denied, nor shall we if it can be avoided. Indeed, to call the deliveries of sense the stuff of knowledge seems to us the clearest procedure in a sceptical economy. We might admit that all that we can know is brought to us through the senses, without thereby impairing at all the true knowledge we can and do have of what the senses bring, once what they bring is safely tucked inside the mind. Color and sound and taste and smell and touch — all these as sensations or ideas are actually what we know them to be; but the reason we can say this without doubt is that when and as known they are all qualities in the mind. Doubt has arisen only when it was claimed that through the senses we know something beyond the senses, that any or all these qualities combine to make a book, or a nose, which is something more than a combination of ideas and is outside the mind. That doubt the senses have not been able to help us resolve. Can the mind of itself resolve that doubt? After what has been said, you almost certainly join me in doubting that it can: the senses are its servants, yes; but a grand dame without servants is hardly more than ornamental — and not always that. But we ought not refuse or hesitate to give mind a chance to show its powers unaided, if such it have.

It is something, at any rate, to be able to acknowledge that the mind certainly knows what is in it. If we could get enough inside it, it could then know all we need to know. One great school of modern thinkers, the idealists, have indeed taken this very tack and have tried to put *every-thing* inside a mind-like receptacle and thus get rid of all doubts. They have usually found, alas, that just before the last load was to be dumped into mind, the human mind, one size too small to hold everything, ran over, spilling its precious burden into an absolute mind, which, while by definition big enough to hold all that overflowed and everything else, grew thereby just one size too large for our limited minds ever to comprehend. Uncomprehended,

> In the monarch's Thought's dominion
> It stood there!
> Never seraph spread a pinion
> Over fabric half so fair.

Such thinkers as these idealists have, therefore, in the event been reduced to the humiliation of having to content themselves with a vague faith in some objective absolute something, after disdaining at the beginning a faith no more vague in some simple external objects. If such faith of either sort were enough, our recovery from doubt were simple at the beginning. For it is easy enough in such a vague sense *to believe* that the book is in your hand and the nose on your face. But belief is not enough if knowledge is by any chance possible. As Descartes says: ' He truly engages in battle who endeavours to surmount all the difficulties and errors which prevent him from reaching the knowledge of truth, and he is overcome in fight who admits a false opinion touching a matter of any generality and importance.' It takes knowledge to cure scepticism completely. Faith is an exaggeration, not an antidote, of doubt; it is a whistling in the dark to keep up courage, not the breath of a giant which can dispel the dark. Tennyson but spoke what is literally true in declaring that there is more faith in honest doubt, believe him, than in half the creeds.

Now, my puzzled reader, any moment you think that you can content yourself with only as much knowledge as is in your mind, you can get rid of doubt — and me together.

> The soul selects her own society,
> Then shuts the door.

You shut yourself in as Emily Dickinson thus advises and I'll heed her further poetic plea in defence of your soul's majesty, and pledge you that I'll

> On her divine majority
> Obtrude no more.

And not only I. No cautious critic will deny you all you claim of certainty, if you thus pay the price of complete solitude. If you're that modest, you are in truth hereafter monarch of all you survey.

23

But no philosopher finds himself all the time to be as modest as that in his demands for certain knowledge. It takes a poet wounded in love or a man in whimsical mood thus to make the great renunciation and fling himself into that well of loneliness. And before you yourself, my reader, win your right to leave us critical philosophers in the lurch, victims of our own exorbitant demands, you must be sure that your own demands are as modest as this. Answer me, for a test, this simple question: Are you willing to admit that your dearest friend is only an idea in your mind? Stay, one thing more: Certify that also of your dearest enemy! Of both, you say? Then I'll take it for granted that you can swallow the world without gulping; and now with a pride not untinged with sorrow I hand you these credentials certifying you as the only self-satisfied solipsist outside the insane asylum. Solipsism, you of course know, is the philosopher's dear name for that belief as luring and yet as fatal to him as the snake's mouth to the fluttering bird, the belief that one's mind and its ideas are literally all there is to the universe itself. It is a lonely way you have chosen, so lonely that the philosopher does not dare it, even when most tempted thereto. Bertrand Russell, who admits that he has looked down this deep well of loneliness only to draw back in fascinated dismay, says that he ' once received a letter from a philosopher who professed to be a solipsist, but was surprised that there were no others! ' No, you are not allowed, for a reason I hope you see, to be surprised that there are no others: you alone are real. Nevertheless, you have as the price of solitude the definite assurance that all that you think you know, you actually know; for you actually know your own ideas, and your own ideas do exist and are all that exists.

What's that? You're handing me back the credentials? So! I thought you would when you understood the matter. Then, you'll face with us philosophers whatever doubt must be braved, rather than brave the gallant way of ' the Ego and his Own.'

V. KNOWLEDGE WITHOUT SENSE USELESS

Prepared, then, to brook despair with us, please face with me, first, one more hope, the last one I have the heart to disclose and then dash. I will not hold out the hope, though some philosophers would, that concepts reveal true external reality, even though all percepts fail us. I would rather simply class percepts and concepts together as ' ideas ' and admit that the failure of the one to lead us to certain knowledge beyond itself is the failure of the other also. Ideas can themselves be truly known, but they cannot assure us that the things beyond the mind for which they claim to stand are real in the same sense as they are.

25

Nor will I hold out the hope that emotions reveal a reality beyond themselves. I trust the head much further than I do the heart, when it comes to the issue of certain knowledge. Those who recommend emotions as means to true knowledge — and there are a few philosophers who do — are grasping the wave itself as their last straw.

There is, however, one more hope that I am willing to propose. It is that, though ideas cannot vouch for objects beyond the mind, judgments (made up as they are of two or more ideas put together by the mind) may reach through to truths that lie outside the mind. You have heard, and most probably have believed, that there are ' self-evident truths.' Our forefathers, for instance, held, in the Declaration of Independence, certain ' truths to be self-evident.' Others have held that judgments of the external world, or of God, are self-validating. It is that sort of hope to which the present discussion turns. If there be truths that actually exist outside minds, and they evidence themselves so that we need have no doubt of their being true, we could through them save from the wreck of doubt enough beliefs for our comfort.

It must be said at once, however, that though such a notion is appealing in our dilemma of doubt, it is a notion very hard clearly to understand, not to say accept. Such truths to meet our

need would have to be more than statements as to
what is inside the mind; for our problem is not met
by mere knowledge of ideas in the mind. We
have exempted that, but we need more than that
for our comfort. How, for a fact, can judgments
that two or more things are related as subject
and predicate get us outside the mind when all
the things we are able to talk about have proved to
be either qualities inside the mind or have remained subject to doubt? Certain it is that the
beliefs mentioned in the Declaration of Independence are no longer regarded as self-evident:
many people never believed them true, and more
would now refuse to believe them. Worse than
that for any real hope in this quarter, the mind in
our generation most like the great minds of our
Founding Fathers — I refer to the mind of Justice
Oliver Wendell Holmes — goes so far as to record
the conviction that ' no concrete proposition is
self-evident, no matter how ready we may be to
accept it.'

But it may be observed that the distinguished
jurist says ' concrete proposition.' Whether he
uses the term ' concrete ' advisedly I do not know,
but we ought not to presume in such a matter.
Are there *abstract* propositions about things outside the mind which are self-evidently true? To
have it so, there would presumably have to be
abstract entities outside the mind to serve as subjects and predicates of propositions; for the propo-

sitions are themselves what the mind makes when it judges. But if what it judges can be shown to be outside the mind, then the judgments might possibly have their truth independent of the mind. This, however, is just the condition that we have not been able to make out with reference to concrete things; for they all upon analysis turn into qualities and slip back into the mind. Have we, then, any way of proving for abstract entities what we have failed to prove for concrete objects?

It seems a hazardous matter, but it has been maintained by some philosophers. Into their involved arguments we cannot here go. But let us illustrate in a more simple fashion the sort of question at issue. Do we not say that 2 plus 2 make 4? Do you acknowledge the statement true? Is it self-evidently true? You may hesitate at that form of question, but anyhow you'll pretty certainly agree that it is plainly true. Do you think of the 2 and 2 as abstract or concrete? You'll see that while the numbers might mean apples, or books, or anything else, the proposition is true regardless of what they mean. In a word, it is true *no matter what*. Now when a proposition is true in that general, or abstract sense, it might be called self-evidently true. But the term ' self-evident ' does not add anything; it merely means that the statement is plainly true. It does ordinarily, however, seem to add something; it seems to relieve the mind of any responsibility in the matter, and to guarantee the delivery of truth in a package all wrapped in celophane. Such suggestions are false and misleading. ' Self-evident ' could not mean that a proposition's truth is evident to *its* self, for it is not a self but just a proposition. It might mean, however, true to *any* and *every* self; true, as we have suggested, no matter what, no matter who.

Now, statements that are true in that sense, however we describe them, still leave us with the question as to whether they exist outside the mind, whether they indeed tell us anything about the universe itself, or merely tell us something about the mind. The latter is the safer guess, for we have seen that the mind may be allowed to know everything that is in it, objects as well as truths. I am here, however, out of my depth; and do not want to dogmatize. Philosophers, after centuries of debate, are still divided upon the merit of this issue of objective truths and of forms or abstractions beyond the mind. When numbers, like our ' 2,' become just numbers as distinct from what is numbered, like our ' apples,' etc., they can easily be thought of as mere ideas confined to the mind. But some great philosophers, notably Plato, have believed numbers to be more objective than anything else, and have thought the mind able to make judgments that in connecting with them proved themselves true in an objective sense. Even these wise men, however, have generally ad-

mitted that from such certain knowledge, however evident it might be, we cannot by any royal
road get certain knowledge about such concrete
things as we have made the lowly basis of our
scepticism. Plato himself said that such pure
knowledge is not becoming to man, and is not
by itself of practical use.

It is in the field of mathematics where most
hope has existed for finding and founding this most
certain truth. Bertrand Russell, whom no one will
accuse of not knowing a thing or two about mathematics, has nevertheless defined it as ' the science
in which we never know what we are talking about
nor whether what we are saying is true.' In such a
field, my reader, you will probably feel as incom-
petent as I feel. If so, let us agree that in our
quest for certain truth we've got ourselves so far
from the facts in which we are primarily interested that we do not know our way about. Let
us return to familiar things, even though not infallibly known. Even certainty in the high realm
of mathematics is admitted not to make certain
our knowledge of things more mundane.

In such realms as politics, religion, economics
we must depend upon other reliances than self-
evident truths. There are few beliefs on the concrete level that are evident to all selves alike. Indeed, the claim that this or that one is self-evident
is seldom if ever heard save in such a situation as
actually refutes it. Men generally appeal to self-

evidence, as was true of the Declaration of Independence, when a quarrel is on, when the quarrel has reached an impasse, and when only one other thing remains to be said before the argument passes into a fight. At that juncture, a nervous disputant may be heard to cry in a shrill voice: ' I tell you that it is self-evident! ' There is no point to the claim in any other situation, and in that situation it is useless. Only undisputed things are seen alike by everybody, and of such things there is no need to assert self-evidence.

If you want further confirmation of this fact, look for a moment at our predicament regarding the class of qualities most important to our peace of mind. Look at Goodness and Beauty. We feel fairly sure early in life that what we think is beautiful *is* beautiful and especially that which is ugly *is* ugly. And if that be true of beauty, how much the more true of our moral notions. We are willing to sacrifice our property and the other man's liberty or even life on the rightness of our judgments of what is right or wrong. But what seems at the beginning so self-evident as to be a matter of honor grows in the urbane man so relative as in the one case, if not indeed in the other, to be a matter of taste, about which it is said that there is no (fruitful) disputing. Your self-evident beauty will easily seem to another a vulgar prejudice tolerable only because it is so obviously subjective. And, as has been said regarding morals,

31

few things are so right that somewhere they have not been believed wrong; and few things so wrong that they have not sometimes been reverenced as finally right. With Kipling, indeed, —

And the wildest dreams of Kew are the facts of Khatmandhu,
   And the crimes of Clapham chaste in Martaban.

VI. COME, THEN, LET US HOPEFULLY EMBARK UPON DOUBT

It has seemed necessary thus to belabor the point in order not to appear arbitrary in declaring that our last hope as proof against elemental scepticism is itself but doubt adorned in words. Whatever may be true of abstract concepts and general judgments, the world at our feet, which we love and would know, turns out, for all they give us, to be either something in our minds or quite unknown. We cannot contentedly admit it all to be inside our minds; so we must at once believe and doubt that it is outside us. Belief and doubt when thus held together, as they always are, give birth in us to wonder, which, as Plato says, ' is the feeling of a philosopher.' If you have come with me, then, gracious reader, all this way, you are now a philosopher; and for better or for worse you will, never doubt, always remain a philosopher. We shall hereafter make the most of our predicament together.

True, we have barely touched as yet upon what

32

philosophers require volumes to discuss. This, indeed, is to be another volume added to the many;
but, as you already discern, this volume is written
to you rather than to any other philosophers. I
hold you, my reader, to be the most important
thing in the world, next to me. You and I together — and we're going together from here on,
you know — are by common consent the all-
important pair. We are more important than our
doubts, than even our hopes. I am willing to leave
abstractions to the technical philosophers this trip,
in order the more solicitously to attend you. True,
in successive chapters I shall be telling about this
philosopher or that, but I'll not forget that I'm
telling it to you. You are yourself a philosopher,
never forget that; but you are interested in life
as well as in thought. Life itself has presented
you with doubts of many sorts. I have only intensified some of these doubts. With malice I've
done it, but not a malice untinged with charity.

For if you'll actually go on through with me,
I am going to treat this whole matter of scepticism
constructively. As against the older notion of
doubt as ' devil-born,' I hold that he who doubts
not is fossilized already. But you have doubted.
Doubt is necessary to life, but life is more than
doubt. The acid of scepticism, once swallowed,
is capable of eating your insides out. But we'll
attend to that. I will promise you no panacea,
for I have none. No panacea is worth its

price. But there are antidotes — in fuller self-understanding and in freer social-sharing. In seeking those, I hazard, we shall find not a few golden compensations for the lowly life of doubt. As we proceed, comfort yourself with this thought: he who sleeps on the floor cannot fall out of bed.

CHAPTER II

DOUBTING ONE'S WAY TO SELF AND GOD

Being a moral from René Descartes et al.

Regarding ancient scepticism, my dear reader, I have in the first chapter hazarded the guess that it was a widespread personal reaction to an even more widespread cultural dissolution. It was a withdrawal of personal participation from a dying order. I called it negative, because it seemed primarily a withholding rather than a relaunching of effort. Greek genius stood with bowed head, as it were, on the summit of Olympus and watched the glowing sunset of a brilliant day, the brightest day of human genius thus far. The day had, indeed, been so bright and the gloaming of that day reflected so fully the dying splendor that the faint stars of another order were not yet shining through.

And yet those stars were there, and they in turn would share the sky with a brighter moon and the whole galaxy of heaven would after the night welcome a new sun and the reborn glory of another day. It is our theme, you remember, that doubt is

35

creative as well as destructive. Our ancient sceptics, however, were caught in motion by the camera
of time, both feet still planted in the old. Their
earth, however, as Thornton Wilder so presciently
puts it in his *Woman of Andros,* ' sighed as it
turned in its course; the shadow of night crept
gradually along the Mediterranean, and Asia was
left in darkness. . . . Triumph had passed from
Greece and wisdom from Egypt, but with the
coming on of night they seemed to regain their
lost honors, and the land that was soon to be
called Holy prepared in the dark its wonderful
burden.'

But the night finally passed; morning came to
herald Christianity as wonderful but not burden-
some. The sun of a new day brought healing
for a weary world in its rays. But the order of
faith, which was thus ushered in, itself in time
grew old and numb. Humble religious experience
passed into Christian doctrine, doctrine matured as
philosophy; and the philosophy of the Schoolmen
hanged itself in a noose of words — words none
the less lethal for all their logical perfection.
When thought reaches its completeness, no room is
left for growth. As the best in aspiration is often
the enemy of the better, so perfection in form is
often enemy of an evolving life. Around the for-
bidding crawfish, I have sought in limping verse
to voice this always recurring elegy of human
aspiration:

Far down within the slimy mire the crayfish works his spell,
To weave around him silently an ever hardening shell.
Such as bequeaths his softness to the mud where it belongs,
And fits himself to take his place with toilers brown and
  strong.

But once his shell is fully grown, his early end attained,
He finds all further growth denied by that already gained.
Then face he must anew the travail of rebirth,
Or find his goal become his doom through the encrusting
  girth.

I. In Quest of a Pathway to Truth

Now René Descartes, the major hero of our
present tale, lifts a tentative voice to descry the
decadence to which mediaeval philosophy had
sunk the Christian life, and even more debased
the fertile fount of common human curiosity.
When men begin to cry their doubts abroad, wise
custodians of culture would look to their foundations. But Bourbons forget nothing, learn nothing. Let me not, however, make easy simplicity
of an age so alien to my own. Descartes himself,
who stood nearer, will unfold the matter more
justly. He knew the sterility of the Scholastic,
that

>He was in Logick a great Critick,
>Profoundly skill'd in Analytick.
>He could distinguish, and divide
>A Hair 'twixt South and Southwest side.

37

He'd run in Debt by Disputation,
And pay with Ratiocination.
All this by Syllogism, true
In Mood and Figure, he would do.

It was indeed just this sterility of method that set Descartes off on a tangent of distrust for his age. What he had learned through this method at the Jesuit college — of La Flèche in Maine — where he was trained, did not leave him happy or his mind satisfied. Yet in reflecting upon the whole matter he had to acknowledge that his was ' one of the most celebrated schools in Europe.' Learned men he had for teachers, nor had he wanted any instruction that other students received. But the disputations which all students alike received as education, were

In proper terms, such as men smatter
When they throw out and miss the matter.

What was actually known in mathematics and morals, not to mention theology, struck him as pathetically small, considering the number of men engaged in study over how long a period; and as for philosophy, spite of its age and distinction, there was, he says, ' not a single matter within its sphere which is not still in dispute, and nothing, therefore, which is above doubt.'

This general disappointment led him, as we shall soon see, to enshrine doubt as the center of his own method. But before we pass to the constructive side, let us note the onus put by him upon the cultural setting that taught for education what could so little satisfy the ambitious mind. Indeed he goes so far as to say that he had ' never observed that any truth before unknown had been brought to light by the disputations that are practiced in the schools.' Their method was indeed so sterile, as he adds, that ' those who have been long good advocates are not afterwards on that account the better judges.' Descartes thought that the educational practitioners prided themselves on having such vague principles and such equivocal procedures as ' enables them to speak of all things with as much confidence as if they really knew them.' ' Such persons,' he elsewhere adds, ' have an interest in my refraining from publishing the principles of the philosophy of which I make use; for . . . I should, by publishing them, do much the same as if I were to throw open the windows, and allow the light of day to enter the cave into which the combatants had descended.'

Discouraged thus with the methods of investigations available, with the results as he saw them in his own case and in that of other contemporaries, ' I found myself,' he confesses, ' involved in so many doubts and errors, that I was convinced I had advanced no farther in all my attempts at learning, than the discovery at every turn of my own ignorance.' He decided at last that he could do no better ' than resolve at once to sweep them wholly away.' Safeguarding action meantime in a manner which we shall remark at the end of this chapter, Descartes elected to intensify doubt, to become, as he put it, ' my own deceiver.'

In coming to so heroic a resolve, Descartes is careful to distinguish his motive and his method from the brand of ancient scepticism already discussed. ' Not that in this,' says he, ' I imitated the sceptics who doubt only that they may doubt, and seek nothing beyond uncertainty itself; for, on the contrary, my design was singly to find ground of assurance, and cast aside the loose earth and sand, that I might reach the rock or the clay.' Nor did he believe that ' the design to strip one's self of all past beliefs is one that ought . . . to be taken by every one.' Descartes had not only been rendered cautious by the fate of Galileo, as he admits in explaining why he deferred publication of his researches, but he was modest and considerate of others. He begins his *Discourse on Method* by declaring that ' Good sense is, of all things among men, the most equally distributed.'

While he was willing to allow to all men the same capacity that he possessed — ' I have never fancied,' says he, ' my mind to be in any respect more perfect than those of the generality ' — he had found something important; and, God helping and the Church not hindering, he could do no other than develop the lead upon which he had stumbled in his groping. Other men, he thought, should act the same way, in the interest of humanity. And while Descartes himself declares that his major aim was to further the progress of medical science and thus be of practical service to men — ' to be useful to no one,' he remarks, ' is really to be worthless ' — nevertheless his great service was the affirmation of a general method more fruitful than any other, the Method of Doubt, being a deliberate effort to balance the inherited prejudices of credulity by those of ' hypothetical ' caution.

II. THROUGH DOUBT TO SOLID GROUND AT LAST

What Descartes really discovered at bottom, or thought he discovered, was that activity requires a substance. He finds himself engaged in the activity of thinking; he concludes that he must exist as a soul substance in order for the activity to exist. Since, however, one kind of thinking is doubting, he is able to state his case as a memorable paradox: doubt of anything doubtlessly implies acceptance of something. I could not doubt unless at least I exist. Whether, then, we stop with the simple *cogito ergo sum* or pass to the *dubito ergo sum,* we seem out of doubt-infected thought to have found an indubitable thinker. Scepticism is not only basically creative, on this view; but it is actually creative of its own cure.

We shall not too much trouble ourselves with Descartes' logic at this stage of unfolding his method, or for that matter at any stage. We must, however, note in passing that subsequent thinkers have not been as certain as Descartes that think*ing* (the activity) implies a think*er* (as substance). Indeed to say that *I think therefore thinking is; I doubt therefore doubting is,* would seem to be a more cautious and safe line of reasoning than Descartes'. But this would not prove what Descartes needed to meet his particular doubt. He wanted a substance on which the more substantially to stand, and so he passed from rational activity to a rational actor; and so passing, was assured, to his own satisfaction, of the existence of his own self, ' a substance whose essence or nature consists only in thinking.'

Here arises, therefore, the first fruit of doubt — a self. Without doubting, there might be a soul, but there could be no assurance of a soul. At the very lowest, doubt creates assurance; assurance is in very truth doubt-born. Without doubt it would simply never arise. But, you may well urge, why is not acceptance, a state preceding doubt, better than assurance, a state succeeding doubt? I ask you in turn, why is innocence not better than character? The answer in both cases is the same: innocence, though beautiful, is at the mercy of events beyond its control; character is itself so far forth a control of events. Acceptance, likewise, can maintain itself in a changing world only by passing into assurance. Life inflicts uncertainty upon us humans and doubt is the technique we have of converting it into assurance. Nor is assurance so far forth at the mercy of events; it has met its problems in advance and so possesses poise upon their every reappearance. Only by passing through doubt can one transcend it; and only by transcending it, taking it up into one's responses, can one stably stand against a world which itself, willy-nilly, threatens at any moment to throw us into the fever of doubt. No immunity here without inoculation; but fairly dependable immunity through inoculation.

A soul, however, did not seem to Descartes enough. Foundation only it was; how provide the superstructure? A mind shut up merely with certain knowledge of its own ideas, we too have dismissed as not enough. The mind wants a world; and Descartes, facing in advance the problem I thrust upon you in Chapter I, found God as the guarantor of the quest for assurance as to the external world. The matter developed, according to his own report, in the following manner.

Finding in himself not only thoughts of doubt by which he could prove his existence as a thinker, Descartes found in himself thoughts of perfection by which he could prove the existence of superior perfection outside himself. With the same clearness and distinctness whereby the self was established through doubting, Descartes was assured that something cannot come from nothing. It is as unthinkable, he argued, that the better could come from the worse as that something should come from nothing. In order to explain therefore the presence in us of ideas of a perfection which itself we do not have, a being more perfect than we must be assumed. But we find in us not merely ideas of a perfection greater than we; we find indeed the idea of a being than whom no more perfect can be conceived. Such a being must exist to cause in us such an idea. He must also exist to cause us; for if we could have caused ourselves we would have made ourselves with the virtues we now attribute to God.

Descartes does not recognize in this discrepancy a reflection upon God; for he reasons the other way around, that since God must be perfect to explain our ideas of perfection, the fact of our imperfections cannot be blamed on God. He is able to get rid of other more detailed doubts also in short order. The goodness of God proves him unwilling to deceive us, and so we can depend upon the clearness and distinctness of any and all ideas to guide us to truth and away from error. Whatever, therefore, we clearly and distinctly perceive to be so, *is* so, though Descartes acknowledged ' that there is some difficulty in rightly determining the objects which we distinctly perceive.'

Indeed, this quality of clearness and distinctness in ideas as test of their truth proved as inconclusive for Descartes as has the principle of self-evidence for others. When it proved enough, it was always in danger of proving too much. Take dreams, for instance, often embarrassingly distinct and vivid. ' How do we know,' queried Descartes himself, ' that the thoughts which occur in dreaming are false rather than those others which we experience when awake, since the former are often not less vivid and distinct than the latter? ' Descartes worries not a little over this matter. It threatened his salvation from doubt.

After entertaining all available hypotheses regarding it, he reached the high-handed position once of simply having ' reason dictate that, since all our thoughts cannot be true because of our partial imperfection, those possessing truth must infallibly be found in the experience of our waking moments rather than in that of our dreams.' Again he relied upon the continuity furnished by memory in waking moments as against the discontinuity of dreams. Not on such, however, is Descartes' final reliance, but on God; for, as he says, ' though men of the highest genius study this question as long as they please, I do not believe that they will be able to give any reason which can be sufficient to remove this doubt, unless they presuppose the existence of God.' He makes perfectly clear in this same connection that natural reliances for removing doubt, such as clarity and distinctness, are themselves infected with doubt save for the dependence upon God. Grant God, however, with his power and perfection, and back comes the world and all that is in it much as before the onset of doubt. Doubt God, and nothing remains certain save the self established by the fact of doubting. Since the self and its dreams were not enough for Descartes, the full creativeness of scepticism depended upon removing the existence of God from all doubt.

Early modern thought was as a whole so much of the same opinion, that we ought not to rest the case for God against doubt merely with Descartes. His rescue of the soul from doubt was a stroke of genius. I do not mean that it was entirely original with him (Augustine had suggested it), or that it completely proved the case; but as inventions go in the realm of spirit Descartes' *cogito ergo sum* was of the order of genius. It was a great creative thrust of human scepticism. But his rescue of God from scepticism resembles more a work of desperation. The easy way in which he exonerates God from blame for evil as well as the easier way he commends for the faithful the adequacy of reasoning in a circle, but reflect the impetuosity of the argument which we have already examined. Evil he tries to blame off on our wills and other imperfections, though God has been shown to be all-powerful and no effect to exist without an adequate cause. The theological proof of God's existence

46

from the Bible, after assuming that the Bible is trustworthy because it comes from God, is declared ' true ' for the faithful, ' nevertheless this cannot be submitted to infidels, who would consider that the reasoning proceeded in a circle.'

All this makes it probable that Descartes never suffered profoundly from religious scepticism, whatever his scientific qualms may have been. His doubt was more a logical method than it was a personal misery. And with his soul assured, he did not canvass every inch of the way from soul to God. It was as though his secure soul did, rather, amuse

> . . . her self with doubts profound,
> Only to show with how small pain
> The sores of faith are cured again.

The creative aspect of scepticism with reference to God was earlier treated by St. Anselm of the 11th century and more concretely by Bishop Berkeley of the 18th century. Anselm is the first adequately to broach the argument from the peculiar nature of the idea of God to the necessity of his existence. Berkeley makes very dramatic the dire predicament of a man who seeks to go it alone, without God. It will further clarify and dignify Descartes' method of doubt if we turn for a moment to these thinkers. And first Anselm.

III. ANSELM'S BOLD STROKE AGAINST DOUBT

Saint Anselm, Archbishop of Canterbury, tells us feelingly of the pains through which he achieved the audacity to say: ' I do not seek to understand that I may believe, but I believe in order to understand. For this also I believe, — that unless I believed, I should not understand.' Anselm was of course always possessed of an acceptance of God, but he wanted more than mere acceptance; he wanted assurance, and particularly the means of conclusive assurance of others. He describes his state of mind after he had already written one book, *Monologium,* upon the existence and nature of God. That is, after he had made more or less the usual arguments. ' I began,' says he, ' to ask myself whether there might be found a single argument which would require no other for its proof than itself alone. . . . At last in despair I was about to cease . . . One day, when I was exceedingly wearied . . . in the very conflict of my thoughts, the proof of which I had despaired offered itself.'

What Anselm found, reassuring to many a man since, is called the ontological argument. It consists in proving existence of at least one object of knowledge from the existence of the idea of the object. We do well, perhaps, to put this famous proof in Anselm's own words: ' Even the fool is convinced that something exists in the understanding at least, than which nothing greater can be con-

48

ceived. . . . And assuredly that than which nothing greater can be conceived, cannot exist in the understanding alone. For suppose it exists in the understanding alone: then it can be conceived to exist in reality; which is greater. Therefore, if that than which nothing greater can be conceived, exists in the understanding alone, the very being than which nothing greater can be conceived, is one than which a greater can be conceived. But obviously this is impossible.'

Now, without a doubt, that really seems too good to be true: to be able to pass without a bobble from the mere idea, surrounded with doubt as to whether it is more than idea, to the indubitable object of the idea. This is a thing men long have sought. It is a shortcut to assurance, and one cannot wonder at the elation of Anselm upon discovering it. Others had felt it, and had vaguely tried to declare it. But he for the first time gets it clearly out before us. God would not be God if he did not exist; for the idea of God minus existence is not as great an idea as with existence. But we start with the notion of God as a being than whom no greater can be conceived. Then this very God exists, and no further ifs and ands about it whatsoever.

Is it not for a fact too good to be true? So thought a contemporary of Anselm, a monk, Gaunilo by name. He drew up a sort of analogy to reveal the weakness of the argument. He had in mind, he said, the idea of an island than which no more excellent island could be conceived. Must not the island exist — out there in the ocean? Must it not, since its existence added to its idea would increase its excellence and since by definition the island of our talk has all the excellencies there are? And yet it is not out there. Indeed, ' If a man should try to prove to me by such reasoning that this island truly exists,' said Gaunilo, ' and that its existence should no longer be doubted, either I should believe that he was jesting, or I know not which I ought to regard as the greater fool, myself . . . or him.' So perfect an island is lighted only by that light which never was on any sea.

Anselm let himself out rather lightly from the analogy of Gaunilo; because, as he says among other things, Gaunilo was one of the faithful and did not himself mean to call in question the existence of God. And yet if the island proved by the argument to be out there, is *not* there, the disillusion is certainly calculated to cast reflection not necessarily upon the existence of God but at least upon the means of assurance that Anselm provided. Anselm of course admitted from the beginning that, though his argument would not apply to islands or other mundane objects, it nevertheless indubitably proved God to exist. Since, however, it could be shown not to apply to anything but God, how could he be so sure that it applied even there?

What has merely the advantage of being beyond disproof does not thereby achieve its
proof.

Descartes was more sensitive to this objection
than was Anselm. He had the advantage of several
succeeding centuries of criticism. He uses the
same argument, as we have seen. While, to use
language later applied to the argument by John
Locke, Descartes does not out of ' over-fondness
for this darling invention cashier ' all other arguments, he puts some stead upon it, nevertheless.
He substitutes in his formulation of it the notion
of perfection for Anselm's notion of greatness,
though Anselm implied perfection in his term
' great.' Descartes, as we have seen, thought that
he could prove a more perfect than man as source
of those ideas in man's mind more perfect than is
man. For since no stream rises higher than its
source, the fact that we have the notion of any perfection which perfection we ourselves lack, shows
that there must be that perfection existing somewhere to furnish us with the idea of it. This would
necessitate a god as cause to explain the idea of
him as effect in our minds.

But such was not enough for Descartes. His
general method called for clear and distinct ideas
as the final test of truth of every kind. Now just
any god might fool us while we are awake, as he
permits us to be fooled while we are asleep. Indeed, how do we know that life itself is not an

alternative set of dreams to those of sleep? Descartes saw no way of answering these questions save to add to God's existence a moral perfection past any suspicion of deception. This perfection, added for this reason, becomes available in turn to prove from the mere idea the existence of such a being — a being than whom none more perfect can be conceived.

Let us divert ourselves for a moment before finishing Descartes' view of this whole matter. The beauty of this ontological principle is that it seems to prove one thing about as well as another, provided only superlatives be used in the right places. Suppose, for example, we try our hand at proving the devil. I say ' the ' devil, dear reader, well knowing that you would not be willing for us to deliver to you at that end of the line a little insignificant devil. You'll expect great things of us, in keeping with the tradition about the argument, if we turn our hand to this nefarious matter. So we'll order a regular devil. The magnificent is for language hardly more difficult than the puerile. In truth, the devil in our estimation is a being than whom no more devilish an imp can be conceived. Now, surely, devilishness that actually exists is more devilish than devilishness that exists merely in imagination. Otherwise those of us who just arm-chair our way into deviltry are as bad as Dillinger — or whomever you will. Oh, that Miniver Cheevy, for the deviltry of his soul, could have been such a philosopher! You remember E. A. Robinson's lines . . .

> Miniver loved the Medici,
>   Albeit he had never seen one;
>   He would have sinned incessantly
>   Could he have been one.

Now if you've been watching closely, I think you'll agree that we have proved our devil to exist. True, we've taken it easy to give you relief from Anselm; but the devil whose devilishness does not actually exist is simply not the devil of our definition. We've ordered a perfect imp of a devil, and got him — a devil than whom for an actual fact none could be conceived more devilish.

Now it was advisedly that I said above that this line of thought ' *seems* to prove one thing about as well as another.' Descartes addresses himself even more specifically than does Anselm to the task of showing that this is not the case. Believing himself that ' thought imposes no necessity on things,' Descartes is cautious: ' as I may imagine a winged horse, though there be none such, so I could perhaps attribute existence to God, though no God existed.' The cases, he goes on to argue, are not the same: existence can be proved from conception only in those cases where you cannot have the conception without existence. ' And God is the only such case. Because I cannot conceive God unless as existing, it follows that existence is inseparable from him, and therefore that he really exists: not that this is brought about by my thought, or that it imposes any necessity on things, but on the contrary, the necessity which lies in the thing itself, that is the necessity of the existence of God, determines me to think in this way, for it is not in my power to conceive a God without existence, . . . as I am free to imagine a horse with or without wings.'

You will have to judge, my reader, whether there remains about this argument in spite of the defense of both these ingenious thinkers (and others not mentioned here) an air of unreality. If you decide to allow the argument to stand, I am, I remind you, myself pretty partial to my argument for the devil, that is, for a real he-man devil. But it is not my chief task here, or in this book as a whole, to pass final judgment upon the several resolutions of doubt offered by the thinkers discussed. To be sure, I shall not go out of my way to avoid expressing opinions upon the validity of their resolutions, but I set little stead upon criticisms of others in this book. (I have undertaken this critical task in another book, *Beyond Conscience*.)

What in this book I set myself to make clear through the examples of others is the rôle that doubt plays in the creative life. Let us not ask primarily whether the cures for doubt proposed by others are satisfactory to us. The doubts were theirs; theirs the cures. Let us see how they cured their ills. It is really too much to ask them to cure

54

our doubts; they did well if they cured their own.
Doubt must be recurrent, if the creative life is to
continue. As the Anglo-Saxon bard said at the end
of each stanza of his hero's woes, ' His troubles
passed away; so will mine.' It is in that spirit that
we here parade the doubts and cures for doubt of
other men. If doubt must arise, if once arisen it can
be cured, if the cure of it leaves the doubter upon
a higher level, creating not only assurance otherwise lacking but many valuable by-products also
— then it is enough for us to illustrate the process
in order to nerve us to face with hope our own
doubts, whatever they may be.   In this sense,
Anselm and Descartes are among the heroes of the
race, whatever we think of their acceptances, their
doubts, or their doubt-engendered assurances.

IV. A Bishop Sets a Snare for Sceptics

Let us turn, however, from this rather abstract
way of guaranteeing God and examine Bishop
Berkeley's more concrete method.   Even Berkeley's way may not seem to you the simplest manner
of mastering your own doubts, if any, upon the
matter at hand. But Berkeley thought that he had
literally reduced philosophy to its lowest, most
human terms. He claimed really to bring at last
together in a happy union the views of common
men and those of the philosophers; for, argued he,
common men always claim that we know real

things; and the philosophers have shown us that what we know are ideas. The conclusion is then easy enough: *real things are ideas.* But where does God come into all this?

Well, he comes in at just the right pinch. If we may defer his entrance until the dramatic moment, we acknowledge meantime that it was from Bishop Berkeley that we got the ideas and most of the arguments in our first chapter. We started with sound, you remember, and let everything else follow sound into the mind, until there seemed nothing left in the universe save mind and its sensations, ideas, conceptions, judgments. Now the good Bishop did all this very systematically and he did it with such ingenuity that he drove the great Dr. Samuel Johnson to distraction and violence (of kicking the stone to disprove it), as we meant to drive you to humility. Berkeley did all this with a pious motive, as the full title of his *Three Dialogues* indicates: ' the design of which is plainly to demonstrate the reality and perfection of human knowledge, the incorporeal nature of the soul and the immediate providence of a deity in opposition to sceptics and atheists.' But all this he did very convincingly, as this sketch of his argument will suggest.

He starts with the quality of heat, as we did with sound. But extreme heat is admitted to be pain, which is surely something in us rather than in the object. A more moderate degree of heat, warmth, is pleasure, which equally must be held to be in us rather than in the object. If, however, you insist that heat, or cold, is in the object, you are asked to reflect upon the fact that a thing cannot be both hot and cold at the same time, as water seems to be when you put into it one hand that is hot and the other hand that is cold. The simplest way out of all this is to admit the truth, that heat and cold are sensations in the mind.

After heat and cold are both made ideas in the mind to avoid an absurd world, there follow by the same logic tastes, odors — and this segment of the dialogue, which puts us again on ground most familiar:

' *Philonous.* It seems then there are two sorts of sound — the one vulgar, or that which is heard, the other philosophical and real?

Hylas. Even so.

Phil. And the latter consists in motion?

Hyl. I told you so before.

Phil. Tell me, Hylas, to which of the senses, think you, the idea of motion belongs? to the hearing?

Hyl. No, certainly: but to the sight and touch.

Phil. It would follow then, that, according to you, real sounds may possibly be *seen* or *felt*, but never *heard*.

.   .   .   .

Hyl. To deal ingenuously, I do not like it. And, after the concessions already made, I had as well

57

grant that sounds too have no real being without the mind.'

All qualities follow these, in Berkeley's extremely acute reasoning, until belief in matter seems only the superstition of ' you know not what, and you know not why.' If we really do not know ' what ' matter is, then, pray, urged Berkeley, how do we know *that* it is at all? To make short a matter delightfully longer in the three dialogues, we neither know nor have any intellectual grounds for believing that there is any such thing as material substance. As Hylas admits when he reaches the nadir of despair, ' Truly my opinion is that all our opinions are alike vain and uncertain. What we approve today, we condemn tomorrow. We keep a stir about knowledge, and spend our lives in the pursuit of it, when, alas! we know nothing all the while: nor do I think it possible for us ever to know anything in this life. Our faculties are too narrow and too few. Nature certainly never intended us for speculation.'

Upon inspection, then, all the things we know turn out to be in our minds; but since we know real things, the real things are our ideas: *esse est percipi*. But if ' to be is to be perceived,' the world has not only dissipated itself into our ideas, it has lost all its stability in so reducing itself. Reality is as unstable as a dream, in which things come and go at our whimsical beck and nod. With a fancy we create the world; with a slip of memory we forget it out of existence. When we lie down at night to rest, the bed slips out from under us into nothingness the moment we cease to be conscious of it — for not to be perceived is not to be — and our own dear bodies in a dreamless sleep are forgotten into nothingness. Our awakening the next morning is the creation of our selves anew by an aroused self consciousness.

Now this instability of the whole apparently stable order is very disturbing. It is rendered none the better by the fact that other people are swallowed into the mind of each person by the same process that engulfs objects through the suction upon their qualities. This consequence of the logic, however, Berkeley did not emphasize. Nor did he draw the consequence that if material substance is only our perceptions, then *spiritual substance,* the souls that he accepted gratefully from nature and Descartes, are only our *ideas* of them. It remained for Hume to draw this inexorable conclusion from Berkeley's premises, as we shall see in the next chapter.

But we shall discover the final creative aspect of Berkeley's scepticism, if for the moment we focus sharply on his argument. Prepare now to meet God. Having shown that things exist only in a mind, he offers us the choice between the shifty, dream universe created and destroyed by the vagaries of our own mind, orphaned completely from being in dreamless sleep, and the stable, dependable universe created by the perception of a universal spirit and maintained by a continuous mindfulness which never slips a cog by one wink of unconsciousness. Take God, you sceptics out there, or know that the bed slips out from under you the moment you drop off to sleep! That, thought Berkeley, put the sceptics right where he wanted them: between the devil of nothingness and the deep blue sea of God's love and care.

' I conclude,' says Philonous, ' not that things have no real existence, but that, seeing they depend not on my thought, and have an existence distinct from being perceived by me, there must be some other mind wherein they exist. As sure, therefore, as the sensible world really exists, so sure is there an infinite omnipresent Spirit who contains and supports it. . . . You may now, without any laborious search into the sciences, without any subtlety of reason, or tedious length of discourse, oppose and baffle the most strenuous advocate of Atheism.' Now this is a great advantage, indeed, to one who, like Philonous, was ' of a vulgar cast, simple enough to believe my senses, and leave things as I find them.' And Philonous puts the antithesis between this and other methods of proving God in this clear manner: ' Men commonly believe that all things are known or perceived by God, because they believe the being of God; whereas I, on the other side, immediately and necessarily conclude the being of a God, because all sensible things must be perceived by Him.' What, then, in all truth, could be more conclusive, from Berkeley's point of view, than the closing statement of these great dialogues — ' the same Principles which, at first view, lead to Scepticism, pursued to a certain point, bring men back to Common Sense.'

V. Action Shielded from Doubt

But life is short, and between what Berkeley called the ' first view ' and the final conclusion the way was rough — and for most mortals may be long. To go just doubting along this road of life is not so easy or so safe in practice as it sounds in books. Inevitable, but not easy. Some action is necessary in every life, and upon what is action to rest while the season of doubt covers us? To neglect an answer to this question arising from the practical side is surely to neglect something important in connection with doubt, if there actually be any answer.

Fortunately, Descartes has both recommended and provided an answer. It may not be your answer, but it served him and may prove, if cautiously used, an aid to you. But let us now at the end of our study of Descartes get his whole plan before us. Finding that life inflicted doubt upon him, he intensified doubt so as to lessen the prospect of always being fooled, and covered the whole procedure with four resolutions:

1. 'Never to accept anything for true which I did not clearly know to be such.' This was his 'method of doubt,' the methodical conversion of fate into fortune: all done, as we have said in contrasting modern with ancient scepticism, 'to exclude all ground of doubt.'

2. 'To divide each of the difficulties under examination into as many parts as possible, and as might be necessary for its adequate solution.' In this Descartes fathered the scientific procedure of minute division of labor in the intellectual field.

3. 'To conduct my thoughts in such order that, by commencing with objects the simplest and easiest to know, I might ascend by little and little, and, as it were step by step, to the knowledge of the more complex, assigning in thought a certain order even to those objects which in their own nature do not stand in a relation of antecedence and sequence.

4. 'And the *last*, in every case to make enumerations so complete, and reviews so general, that I might be assured that nothing was omitted.'

But before setting out upon this journey from faith disturbed to the finer destination of faith assured, Descartes formulates with the same care as the foregoing, certain rules for the crises of action that may arise. Changing to his own figure, we are to rebuild the house in which we live, because we have outgrown it and must have more commodious quarters. But we must live (in it)

while we are rebuilding it. ' That I might not remain irresolute in my actions, while my reason
compelled me to suspend my judgment, and that I
might not be prevented from living thenceforward
in the greatest possible felicity, I formed a pro-
visory code of morals, composed of three or four
maxims, with which I am desirous to make you
acquainted:

' The *first* was to obey the laws and customs of
my country, adhering firmly to the faith in which,
by the grace of God, I had been educated from
childhood, and regulating my conduct in every
other matter according to the most moderate opinions, and the farthest removed from extremes,
which should happen to be adopted in practice
with general consent of the most judicious of those
among whom I might be living.' This decision
sought to avail itself, through fixing the eye
upon the golden mean of collective wisdom, of a
steadying influence for action while the mind
doubted.

' My *second* maxim was to be as firm and resolute in my actions as I was able, and not to adhere
less steadfastly to the most doubtful opinions,
when once adopted, than if they had been highly
certain.' Action requires firmness for success and
one must subscribe to the conditions of what he
must do, even if arbitrarily so. Action must sometimes be based upon an ' as if,' even though
thought may escape it. And the best ' as if's ' for

action are those that play down the ' if's ' and up the ' as's.'

' My third maxim was to endeavour always to conquer myself rather than fortune, and change my desires rather than the order of the world, and in general, accustom myself to the persuasion that, except our own thoughts, there is nothing absolutely in our power.' This counsel of resignation with reference to what actually lies beyond our power is, no doubt, dangerous; because we can never be certain whether its lying beyond control is remediable by more resolute effort. Though the light for action must here, as elsewhere, be extracted and applied at one's own risk, there is in Descartes' third maxim a mellow wisdom for life. It was in this attitude, Descartes concluded, where chiefly lay ' the secret of the power of such philosophers as in former times were enabled to rise superior to the influence of fortune, and, amid suffering and poverty, enjoy a happiness which their gods might have envied.'

It is the example since Descartes of scientists inspired in no small part by his method, rather than the example before Descartes of the philosophers who inspire him, that gives us pause at taking this third maxim too literally. For these scientists have shown as much resoluteness and equanimity in surmounting the previously thought ' inevitable ' as did the earlier philosophers in accepting it. It is at the limits of control where Descartes' counsel is rightly available, and since these limits are unknown a certain cautious audacity is always advisable as to what the limits of control are. But there are limits, never doubt, and Descartes advises sagely regarding them.

If we may now put in our own terms the final fruit of doubt as developed by Descartes, we shall say (1) that doubt is inevitable, (2) that action is also inevitable, (3) that doubt while it may energize action intended to relieve itself, nevertheless impairs other action, (4) that since, however, we do not doubt everything all at once, we are wise to borrow for necessary action in doubtful fields whatever certitude remains in other fields, and (5) that doubt when had and bravely resolved, rather than weakly downed, enriches future action as it tones the mind itself up from succulent innocence to mellowed assurance. So much we glean from Descartes and his fellows.

You will note how carefully I refrain from saying that we inherit from Descartes a nevermore to be doubted soul and deity. These and other beliefs we must certify for ourselves if they are to become our verities. We cannot on the basis of the method of Descartes tell a man what he must believe after doubt any more than we can tell him not to doubt the beliefs he already has. To tell a man what he must arrive at through doubting is to try to tell him that he must not doubt. It is, however, only to ' try.'

The world in which we live —

> How is this vast world garmented
> As turn on turn it troubles space? —

this troubled world from time to time renders ancient ' truths ' uncouth, and doubt becomes our sign of caution, coming events casting their shadows before. The only way to avoid doubt is to elect to be an idiot; and nature has taken that option out of our hands. No, we cannot borrow or inherit the fruits of Descartes' triumphs, or those of any other man. The profit that is ours from former worry and toil is the acceptance of an inevitability as a potential asset rather than as a necessary liability. Candor puts us in touch with our inheritance, and courage transforms, if anything can, our doubts into faiths befitting our own time and place. Be candid, dear reader, as to uncertainties; have courage, my friend, to stomach your doubts if you cannot see them through to certitude.

CHAPTER III

DOUBTING ONE'S WAY TO SPIRITUAL PEACE

Being a moral drawn from Benedict Spinoza

In none of the philosophers thus far studied has there been no outlet for energy save thought. Anselm was a high official in the church. Berkeley traveled to colonial America to found a college for training Indians and missionaries to Indians, and later became a bishop. Descartes was in his youth a soldier of fortune, and throughout life remained a man of the world. He corresponded with noble ladies, dedicating two of his books to them and dying from inflammation of the lungs caught in early morning vigils as philosophic tutor of Queen Christine of Sweden. Important, that is, as was the speculative venture to each of these, philosophy was not the be-all and the end-all of their personal careers. To see the supreme test of scepticism as a way of life, we ought to investigate the career of a doubter who was shut off from the world and left to live upon the fruits of his own solitude. If we could find one whose ostracism from active life was itself due to his doubt, so much

67

the better test.   Now, it happens that for a sober
fact Benedict Spinoza's life answers rather neatly
to this description.

I. What the World Did to Spinoza

Belonging to a group that up to his time had
been mercilessly persecuted and that in his time
was on sufferance in Holland, whither his community had fled from earlier persecution in Spain
and later persecution in Portugal, Spinoza was by
fate cut off from any close spiritual contact with
the gentile world.   To make his isolation complete,
he was excommunicated from the Synagogue at
the age of 24 after having been trained for the
rabbinate.   Nor was there any family group left
to be his moral support.   The family drove him
from its door upon the excommunication, and a
sister subsequently tried to defraud him of a
patrimony that was legally his.   As an example,
however, of the milk of human kindness that
flowed generally in his veins, let it be remarked
that after having won his legal right to the money
in question, he turned the entire amount over to
the grasper.

Plato, it will be remembered, tells the story of
Gyges, whose shepherd ancestors in a mysterious
cavern discovered a magic ring that enabled him
at will to make himself invisible.   What this man,

in the story, didn't do, is not worth mentioning.
Plato even capped his wickedness with the reputation of a stainless life. What more would one
want? — the spoils of wickedness without danger of detection, and the rewards of righteousness
without any of its pains. But Plato called this
paragon of fortune unhappy. His exact opposite,
moreover, Plato held up as being a happy man,
in spite of his suffering all the penalties of wickedness without even the pleasure of being known for
the good man he actually was. Both Plato's extreme characters were elaborated for the sake of
a moral. But in the fulness of time, Plato's illustration of the just man reaping the opprobrium of
injustice was fairly materialized. Spinoza was
the man.

What he was at heart I have suggested. What
his people did to him I have indicated. But look
you what men have said against this just man, this
' God-intoxicated ' recluse. Colerus, his first biog-
rapher, described Spinoza's philosophy as ' the
most pernicious atheism that ever was seen in the
world.' Bayle, a fellow-philosopher, called him
' the systematizer of atheism.' And David Hume,
whom we are presently to hold up as the king of
all modern sceptics, referred to Spinoza's teaching
as ' the hideous hypothesis of that famous atheist.'
A recent critic (Dr. S. M. Melammed in *Spinoza
and Buddha: Visions of a Dead God*) has made

him out as a deserter of the whole Western way of life and a promulgator in Oriental temper of 'a dead God.'

Was this mild mannered man, this truth seeker, whom men cast off from among them and whom a large segment of history has counted a devil — was he happy, as Plato foretold? Did he fulfil Plato's moral as well as Plato's pattern? Or was he as miserable as mankind has been wont to assume such a man must be? That is a momentous question. So momentous, that it is clear that it has been too much for most religions. They have assumed that the good man must somehow get the goods, hereafter if not here, before he can be happy. One Christian saint has spoken for the great majority of saints in holding that if in this life only we have hope in religion, then of all men are we most miserable. Let us acknowledge at once, however, what the title of our chapter has already committed us to defend, that Spinoza by all standards available to us either won happiness or what many men would regard as better than happiness, peace of spirit.

But note that I said he *won* it. Spinoza differed from many religious people, but not from all — for he himself was a religious man — in seeing that happiness is not a gift, but an achievement. Not even God could make a man happy who had not himself already won the right and prepared the way. Remember Lucifer.

It was some such mood as the foregoing with reference to popular religion that first got Spinoza into trouble with his own people. The exact nature of his early denials is not here essential, but they turned around such notions as that the material world might be the body of God (an idea we shall see broached in modern form by Montague in our Chapter V), that angels might be imaginary beings, that the soul might be life rather than some independent entity, and that the Old Testament was silent on immortality. Spinoza's elders were afraid to allow one of their number to offend orthodox Christian views, as well as Jewish, in a country where after all the whole group were exiles on sufferance. They no doubt thought the matters of moment in themselves also, but reputation seemed to trouble them more than the errors involved. At any rate Spinoza was offered a valuable annuity if he would remain formally loyal to the Jewish faith. But he had the courage of his youthful scepticism, and welcomed the real bleakness of excommunication rather than profess to believe what he did not believe, whatever precisely that may or may not have been.

Kicked out of his community, deprived of his normal profession, deserted by family and friends, he found his very life in danger, escaped slightly wounded, it appears, from an assassin's dagger, and fled Amsterdam to be haunted for the remainder of his life by the fear, when not the fact, of persecution. Having lost his community and having no people to whom he was privileged to go, he, in recognition of his cultural death, changed his name from Baruch to Benedict (exchanging thus a lost hope of parochial for a new hope of universal ' blessedness,' since both names mean just that), accepted solitude as his lot, lived most of his life in penury and not infrequently as a consequence in attics, disdained all offers of money, save at last a pittance from a friend, ground lenses at odd times for a living, declined later in life a professorship at Heidelberg, because he feared loss of private freedom, and died at 45 from the disease that loves the company of attics and attrition. His death left few to grieve but the manuscript of a book destined to grieve many who, unlike himself, put their confidence in suppressive action rather than in the freedom of thought. This manuscript, his famous *Ethics,* got published through a friend when its author, alas for persecutors, was well beyond the reach of fear or malice.

II. Spinoza's Response to the World's Onslaught

But let us be more systematic, beginning now with Spinoza at the bottom and then follow his steps out of the depths. At the threshold of manhood, his world had fallen in ruins around him.

His first response was to intensify the sceptical spirit that had helped produce the ruins. Rejected by his people because he questioned their God, he rejected in toto their God. He rejected even more. He rejected their world, and set out to build him a world which when he could say of it what the old Jehovah had said of *His* world — ' It is good! ' — then would Spinoza *call* his own creation God. Like the old Jehovah, however, he had nothing or next to nothing out of which to build a world. Spinoza had only his ideas. Some of them he knew were fictitious, some false. How to find which were poor and which were good enough to build upon, this was his problem, as it had been Descartes', as it had been Berkeley's, as it had been Anselm's. It was Anselm's solution which in spirit Spinoza's was destined most to resemble, as it was Descartes' in form.

' After experience had taught me,' so begins Spinoza's *Treatise on the Correction of the Understanding,* ' that all things which frequently take place in ordinary life are vain and futile; when I saw that all the things I feared and which feared me had nothing good or bad in them save in so far as the mind was affected by them, I determined at last to inquire whether there might be anything which might be truly good and able to communicate its goodness, and by which the mind might be affected to the exclusion of all other things.' We are now able to document out of his biography

73

those first poignant lines, and out of our own
yearnings to give meaning to his quest for truth.
He goes on to indicate, after putting aside a first
notion that such a search was ' ill advised,' being
likely, he feared, ' to lose what was certain in the
hope of attaining what was uncertain ' — goes on to
indicate, I say, that ' honour and riches ' must be
put aside. In no external things could the soul
find her fulfilment and ease.

Nor yet in the siren voice of fame. Spinoza's
discussion of fame shows him most sensitive to the
opinions of others, and gives us a clue to the
personal tragedy his isolation from men actually
was. But he saw no chance of happiness in fame;
for, with Schopenhauer, ' other people's heads are
a wretched place to be the home of a man's true
happiness.' In Spinoza's own words, ' Fame has
also this great drawback, that if we pursue it we
must direct our lives in such a way as to please the
fancy of men, avoiding what they dislike and seeking what is pleasing to them.' Having dismissed
upon counsel of his best thought the claims upon
him of the external world with all it held, as well
as the world of men with its deep appeal, ' I saw
myself,' says he, ' in the midst of a very great
peril and obliged to seek a remedy, however uncertain, with all my energy; like a sick man seized
with a deadly disease, who sees death straight before him if he does not find some remedy, is
forced to seek it, however uncertain, with all his

remaining strength, for in that is all his hope placed.'

Preparation complete, including rules of conduct to which we shall presently refer, Spinoza sets out to discipline his understanding in the way of truth. He surveys and assesses four ways of knowing. The first is ' hearsay.' Clearly the less of this, the better. The second is ' vague experience,' as he calls it. In this way, he said, he knew, for example, that he would die, that oil is fuel for flame, that water will put the flame out, that man is a rational animal. In short, ' thus I know nearly all things that are useful in life.' While this kind of knowledge is necessary for life, it is not the way to the perfect life that Spinoza sought. The third is inference from one thing to another, such as cause from effect, specific property from ' some general proposition.' He judges this latter kind of knowledge to be ' not adequate.' There remains, then, the fourth, ' *wherein a thing is perceived through its essence alone* or through a knowledge of its proximate cause.' From such a procedure, says he, arrives such knowledge as that ' two and three make five, and that if there are two lines parallel to the same line they shall be parallel to each other.'

The last type is the only true and certain knowledge. This ' mode alone comprehends the adequate essence of the thing, and that without danger of error; and therefore it must be adopted above all others.' The other ways of knowing, while necessary at times for the continuance of animal life in us, are only second bests as means to spiritual goals. It is at once a tribute to his honesty and a testimony to the tragic sense of life as he lived it, that he closes his discussion of this only completely adequate kind of knowledge with the candid admission that ' the things which I have been able to know by this knowledge so far have been very few.'

But we must not mistake confessed lack of quantity of things known thereby for any lack of the quality of certainty, which is much more important. One certain truth of the right kind is worth a thousand dubious ones and worth ten thousand of the wrong kind. Before we turn, however, to his discovery, beyond fictions and falsities, of the solvent case of knowledge, let us note more fully the motivation of Spinoza's quest and the precise rôle the solvent truth was meant by him to play. He wanted the truth, yes. But he himself said in addition that he wanted ' continual supreme happiness.'

Now while happiness may as a matter of fact be conditioned on truth, more or less of it, the quest for happiness is not always so conditioned. But it was so conditioned for Spinoza, because other means of happiness had been refused by him when not withdrawn from him by others. There was a sort of Jehovah-like egoism operative here.

Other people might seek ordinary happiness;
Spinoza demanded a ' continual supreme ' variety.
Elsewhere he describes it as ' blessedness.' Others
might proceed cooperatively toward truth;
Spinoza must find it through his own ideas, and
he must find it indubitably. Not that truth is not
common to all and not that company in the quest
is not precious. ' For the greatest good,' he says,
' is for [a man] to attain to the enjoyment . . .
together with other individuals, if this can be.' ' If
this can be ' — there's pathos in that ' if.' But
each must start from his own ideas, and he can end
there, if he must. If friendly human enjoyment
fails you, you fall back upon the world; if it fails
you, then, like a good Stoic, you take yourself for
better or for worse.

III. SPINOZA'S RECOVERY FROM SCEPTICISM

But which in you is the better, which the worse?
So far as understanding goes, it is clear that fictions and falsities are the worse. Those we must
learn to identify and to avoid. True ideas are the
better, but how shall we find them? Descartes
found one true thing, himself, and fished all the
rest out of that. Berkeley found one true deity,
and built all the rest, including himself, out of
God's ideas. Such a commonplace God, however,
one who thinks and feels, rewards and punishes,
was not for Spinoza. Nor could this lens-grinder

from the assumption of himself get, with Descartes, what was required for his felicity. He must first find an idea that could become 'the standard of truth,' as he put it. Spinoza, you see, is concerned, as are all men whom life has failed, with method. But he sees that ' method is nothing else than reflective knowledge or the idea of an idea; and inasmuch as the idea of an idea cannot be granted unless the idea itself be granted first, therefore the method will not be granted unless the idea be first granted.' But not just any ' idea ' will do for this previous idea, upon which all other ideas depend. That such a basic idea must be ' clear and distinct ' goes without saying; but it must be potent as well as clear; for truth plus happiness is the bill that this ' holy outcast ' (Schleiermacher's phrase) presents the disjointed world that had cast him out.

The reader will now recognize that Spinoza is on the threshold of solipsism. If there are only ideas, then one is as true as another. Given ideas, if we are to escape through them to a real world, we must have some way of knowing which are true. Otherwise putative understanding cannot be made into genuine understanding. If ideas are ' clear and distinct,' says Spinoza with Descartes, they are true. But Descartes had already found this test itself in need of testing. Spinoza relies upon it, but with qualification and with supplementation. Such ideas must be ' positive ' rather

than ' negative.' They are ' simple ' rather than
complex. Clear and distinct ideas, he says, ' seem
to depend absolutely on our power; ' confused
ideas are ' often formed in us against our will.' It
appears also that there can really be only one such
idea as his specifications require. Moreover,
' when its definition is given there must remain no
room for doubt as to whether it exists or not.'

Such a master key, if it could be found, being
itself veritably true in that it would by the last
qualification quoted be an idea of an adequate and
an existing object, could constitute ' the standard
of truth,' which Spinoza sought. ' All its proper-
ties,' he adds, could ' be concluded from its definition.' It would be ' the cause of all our ideas.'
Such an idea and knowledge of its indubitable
object would frustrate doubt regarding all other
ideas; ' for *doubtfulness*,' he says, ' is nothing else
than suspension of the mind concerning some affirmation . . . which we would affirm . . . if something did not appear, which being unknown, our
knowledge of that thing must necessarily be imperfect.' Command of such a key concept would
enable us, he claims, even to circumvent Descartes'
initial fear that some ' deceiving God exists who
deceives us in things which are most certain.'
Such an idea *would*, I suppose, do the latter as
well as the other things; for, not longer to delay
what must be dawning upon every reader, Spinoza
is about to perpetrate our old friend, the ontologi-

cal principle, in order to give us a new if not better deity.

But I'd better introduce you considerately to his momentous conclusion, for you'd not recognize his solvent discovery as God if you have not met this Spinozistic deity before. Recalling all that I have been saying as to Spinoza's method, let me now add in his retrospective phrase that ' as soon as we had knowledge of this method, we say . . . that it would be perfect when we had the idea of a perfect being.' Well, that — and what was thought to follow from it — would be a good addition, of course, to *any* method. We need only add that if having ' the idea of a perfect being ' guarantees you the existence of that being itself — for you remember, that was what was thought by Anselm and others to follow from such an idea — then indeed is all well. Now Spinoza reaffirms this ontological principle from Anselm and Descartes and makes it his cure for general scepticism and his foundation for a personal religion. Speaking of his much needed ' standard of truth,' he says, ' This is, then, a being unique, infinite, that is, all being, and that beyond which nothing can be granted.'

That phrase ' all being,' — note that phrase well. It will give you the clue to the fact that many men who do not believe in God believe in Spinoza's deity. Einstein is the latest, though not likely the last, to exclaim: ' *Ich glaube in Spinoza's*

Gott.' Let us turn now to Spinoza's great book, the *Ethics,* to see what this is which can be called God, but which is at once a simple idea, a self-validating idea, a standard of truth for all other ideas, ' a being unique,' ' all being,' ' that beyond which nothing can be granted.' Frankly, my reader, this is *Substance.* The first sentence in the *Ethics* reads: ' I understand that to be the cause of itself whose essence involves existence and whose nature cannot be conceived unless existing.' The third definition adds: ' I understand Substance to be that which is in itself and is conceived through itself: I mean that, the conception of which does not depend on the conception of another thing from which it must be formed.' These are definitions in which he indulges like any hard-boiled geometer. Later in this book he undertakes to prove in geometrical fashion that ' a true idea must agree with its ideal (Axiom 6), that is (as is self-evident), that which is contained in the intellect objectively ["subjectively," as we would now say] must of necessity be granted in nature.'

Now that is enough both to prove my point and to illustrate perhaps as much as you desire Spinoza's style in his *Ethics.* I am not going into the book as a whole, one of the great and most curious books of all times. It has little, however, to do with ethics; the section from which I have just been quoting on Substance is entitled ' Concerning God '; and in truth it identifies Substance, Nature, and God, making all each, and each everything. In this one-each-and-all there are distinctions of ' attribute ' and ' mode ' highly interesting in their place, but not necessary in this place, our purpose being what it is. Our limited aim, here as elsewhere, is to show how fate precipitated our philosopher into scepticism, to discover how he found his way out, and to draw from his life and doctrine what moral we fairly may for ourselves. The first task as regards Spinoza is done; we shall presently proceed to the last task; but our second task requires yet one thing more to complete it, the account of an interruption which Spinoza suffered in the completion of his great *Ethics*.

The major import of that book is now clear and amounts to this: Spinoza in seeking clarity has found salvation, in seeking truth has discovered blessedness. He has found in Substance, which is divine, what earlier he declared the goal of his great quest, ' the knowledge of the union which the mind has with the whole of nature.' Since Substance is all, the mind is a part of it. If we call it God, a new relation obtains between God and the world, between God and man. It is a relation of whole and part, of substance and attribute, rather than the old relation of creator and created, cause and effect. Though Spinoza, by way of popular speaking, uses all these latter terms, his real thought is best furthered by the former statements. It is a thought worth remembering against the day when Hume (as indicated in our next chapter) engulfs causality in scepticism.

IV. Spinoza's Recovery Interrupted

Before our guide had finished the outworking of this major import of his doctrine, when in fact the *Ethics* was perhaps four-fifths done, Spinoza turned aside for some four years to write another book, very different in import from the *Ethics* and destined not only to delay the completion of the *Ethics* but to defer its publication until after his death. The explanation of this distraction will preface a certain negative moral with which we propose to close this chapter. A clue to the explanation may be found in certain rules that Spinoza, after Descartes, drew up for the guidance of his conduct while he was seeking recovery from scepticism. Let us glance at these rules — they are three — and then we shall consider the book itself, *A Treatise on Theology and Politics.*

The first rule to guide his conduct was, in mode of speaking, to cultivate the populace, and ' thus prepare friendly ears to give us a good hearing when we wish to tell them what is the truth.' The second was to limit indulgence in pleasure to line of duty, that is, to health and work. And the third was ' to seek only enough money or anything else as is necessary for the upkeep of our health and life, and to comply with such customs as are not opposed to what we seek.' Now certain ' customs ' were growing up around him which he thought to be ominously ' opposed to ' what he sought. He sought complete happiness, be it remembered, in communion with the whole of nature, or, if we will, in ' the intellectual love of God.' This required freedom to pursue his vocation, which he took to be the fuller exploration and celebration of this substance-nature-deity constellation. But he sought also, as we recall, ' to attain to the enjoyment of such a nature together with other individuals, if this can be.' This subsidiary aim required freedom of speech and publication (among other things, of his *Ethics*). For, as the first of the foregoing rules indicates, the people must be told the truth about his discoveries in order that, if possible, he might save others and thus achieve company in his blessedness.

The ' customs ' that threatened both these objectives had to do with a developing religious intolerance in Holland. Spinoza felt, and certainly not without reason, that the Protestant preachers, who were not without influence in public affairs about him, were threatening to become the enemies of his larger freedom, as the Jewish rabbis had been of his smaller freedom in his youth. His *Treatise on Theology and Politics* was directed at these enemies of (his) freedom. He wrote a friend that by this volume he hoped to lessen the influ-

ence of the preachers, on whose ' excessive authority and impudence' he blamed the growing
intolerance of liberal ideas and the actual persecution of some of his liberal friends. Though the
book was published anonymously, it was generally
known to be his. It branded him an atheist in
advance of any knowledge of his pantheistic *Ethics*
and doomed that classic, as I have said, to await
his death for its publication.

For his *Treatise* on its religious side was just the
thing to make all the Calvinistic preachers and
their pious parishioners angry. He tried to show
them that he was just as religious as they, which
was surely not an immodest undertaking; but he
thought to do this by writing in the seventeenth
century in Holland what even yet passes as frank
' higher criticism' of the *Bible*. Its obvious result
was to fasten on him, as we have seen, an odious
epithet, which meant then as frequently it does
now, nothing in particular that a man believes but
something in particular that others feel against
him.

On the political side the book was worse, if possible, for achieving its pacific purpose, than on its
religious side. It sought to lessen the power of the
clergy by preaching up the complete supremacy of
political power. This was not calculated to soothe
the feelings of the preachers who naturally prized
the power which they held and who did not mean
to give this power up to any political group other

than themselves. Thomas Hobbes had in England
two decades before undertaken the same polemic
against preachers, though with not quite so liberal
a purpose, I think. Hobbes sought to protect political power from the subversive claims of private
conscience fortified by priestly encouragement,
whereas Spinoza sought primarily to protect freedom of thought and speech against a public order
that was religiously motivated and was as a result
intolerant of heterodox opinion.

Neither of them attacked the church as such;
they both quoted Scripture like the devil; and both
thought that religious leaders were tolerable guides
for ordinary men if only religious men would con-
sult the philosophers before they undertook to lead
the people. The state was to be Allah, and philosophy — speaking naturally enough through Spinoza,
Hobbes, and their kind — was to be Leviathan's
prophet. So much for the negative intent of
Spinoza's political effort. Thus far we have merely
the struggle for power between two classes —
preachers and philosophers — with each side describing all too correctly, I fear, the other's motive
as lust for power. You will remember that in the
seventeenth century the national state was on the
make, and Spinoza and Hobbes, in company with
Machiavelli, whom both admired, simply proved
themselves better prophets than the preachers at
picking the new god for the modern world.

Dropping Spinoza's companions in (dis)honor,

we may say that the positive side of Spinoza's
political philosophy consists then of his elevation
of the secular arm above all else and the justification of power itself as the ground and essence of
social morality. This latter emphasis, which still
retains most of its power to horrify, is the abstract
identification of might and right. It begins in
Spinoza with the simple form of holding that there
is no right without power to assert it; it passes
quickly to the view that it is right, even naturally
right, for one to do and to get whatever he can; and
it culminates in the view that, since the state has
the unified and complete power, whatever it can
successfully command is right, though, if wise, he
argues, it will acknowledge thought and speech to
transcend its effective control. Indeed, Spinoza's
final defense of the rightness of free thought and
speech is the fact that the state really *cannot*,
whereas the individual *can*, operate these mecha-
nisms of minds and mouths. The state has no suppressive right in abridging such freedom, because
it has no power to practice freedom save through
free individuals.

Where the state's power actually belongs, however, Spinoza insists that there its right supersedes
the individual's, i.e., action is without the individual's but within the state's right of control.
This right of the state to dominate includes all
sacred as well as all secular enterprises, and this, as
he says, because ' as justice depends entirely on the

decisions of the higher powers, so no one can be just
and pious who does not live in accordance with
their commands.' He carries this view so far as to
demand the individual's submission to constituted
authority ' though he may even have to act in opposition to what he believes to be right, and to do
what he clearly sees ought not to be done.' Moreover, as he declares elsewhere, ' the form of government which has long obtained in a state ought by
all means to be preserved, and . . . no attempt to
change it can be made without extreme danger of
total ruin.'

This is strong language without a doubt, and
even strange language from one who himself believed in the doctrine of natural rights, upon which
we later were to found this nation by a revolution
without a bad conscience. Indeed, the language
may strike Americans as both so strong and so
strange that we may well be tempted to drop
Spinoza at once as a political guide. If, however,
Spinoza used the doctrine of natural rights in a
manner less to American taste than did Locke and
Jefferson, it must be remembered in his honor that
he made more democratic use of it than did Thomas
Hobbes, who in its name quieted not only rebellion
against tyranny but the voice of private conscience
as well. Spinoza falls between these positions. He
is no political revolutionary, that much is clear.
But he is republican, prizing freedom as the great
good and absolving from outer interference free-

dom of thought and speech. But how, then, could he, who turned from arbitrary power of rabbis and preachers, embrace with such gusto the equally tyrannical power of politicians?

The best that can be said, I believe, for Spinoza as a political philosopher is that he was feeling his way to a distinction between government and sovereignty and intended his deference for sovereignty rather than for government. Governments may err, and so deserve gentle correction. But sovereignty is a different matter; abstractly it never errs, and so cannot be corrected. In its name, indeed, citizens may humbly protest against a government; for sovereignty is by definition the common purpose of all citizens for the good, and so — as Rousseau was later to make very clear — sovereignty is not only our common might achieved through contract, but our common right achieved by pooling all our rationality and virtue. This is the best, I think, that can be said for Spinoza as a natural rights theorist, and it leaves an ethically sanctified sovereignty to be in the world of action the prize of whoever can by chance capture and by strength maintain government. The worst that can be said in this connection is that Spinoza does not keep even this distinction in mind, that indeed it came to his mind as an *ad hoc* defense of a government that happened to be tolerant of his peculiar talents and predisposed to defend what he himself most needed, i.e., freedom of speech.

But a cautious philosopher will hesitate between these extremes of the best and the worst that can be said of another philosopher; the right thing is likely to be neither the best nor the worst. In this case, indeed, the right judgment seems to be this: Spinoza was not primarily interested in political philosophy. He was driven to a political theory by an interruption in what he wanted most to do and what he was best fitted to do. Against his counsel of seeing all things *sub specie aeternitatis,* he was warped out of his own course into a field which his personal experiences had not fitted him well to understand. Jewish religion had officially denied the right to share himself with his own people, and now Christian religion threatened to deny him the right to share even his thoughts with other men. Against such arbitrary religious power he proposed to set up a secular power which, though more kindly disposed to him for the moment in Holland, might just as readily and much more effectively deny the rights for which he contended. A political state claiming as much right as it has might — a claim Spinoza did all he could to validate, investing the claim with even his peculiar type of divine sanction — no longer strikes us as a romantic knight-errant ready to ride and strike in favor of free thought and free speech — no, not after Fascist Italy; no, not after Communistic Russia; no, not after Nazi Germany; no, not even after the observation of *any* state in war time, when divinity, of whatever sort, seems to bestir itself and to move much more freely even than usual from patriotic idea to repressive action.

This easy acceptance of power as the stuff of morality blinded Spinoza to the necessity of a critical accounting of the transfer of sovereignty from a bad to a better sovereign, in which transfer crucial political progress often consists. Since in his theory right is determined and constituted by power, power carries all right; and no distinction remains between governments *de facto* and those *de jure*. No adequate provision is made indeed for the operation of private conscience in the name of morality in the attempt to lessen the discrepancy between sovereignty, which by definition is always just, and governments, which by reputation, seldom are. Unduly appreciative of the statics of power, he seems insensitive to the dynamics of power. His normal preference for the general in thought and for the mathematical in form leads him even when the emphasis is on power to neglect its push and to minimize its poison. We shall prefer a more modern knight-errant when we come in Chapter VI to discuss the relation of doubt to democracy. But Justice Holmes, there to be our guide, has in Spinoza a splendid predecessor in defense of freedom of thought and speech. This emphasis alone would entitle Spinoza to the thanks of civilized mankind.

It happened that these basic liberties were the

forms of power which Spinoza best understood and most highly prized. Through these his own individual will to power manifested itself and upon these intellectual goods which he understood at first hand he made his best political stand. In exercising his own will to triumph, Spinoza sought the privilege of speech without the irksomeness of place; the prestige of recognition without the responsibility of office; the elixir of intellectual leadership without the discouragement of seeing overt action go awry. Though belatedly, these variegated laurels mankind has accorded to him, accorded them on the ground primarily that he achieved the goal he consciously set himself as compensation for mankind's neglect. That goal was a philosophy of life which would do for him what the harassed Synagogue could not and what the triumphant Christian community would not do for him, guarantee him individual blessedness.

We have here the setting for a personal ethics, a philosophy of life, in short a way of salvation; but if we are wise we shall not expect from Spinoza's *Ethics* any social morality of great moment for us today; for the world had denied him the indispensable training in social and political relations from which unwarped social insight could come. Spinoza's mild revenge was the determination to get his own happiness out of his own mind and thus to convict the world of irrelevance. This he did by his withdrawal from the world, and by his subsequent intellectual achievements without substantial aid from others.

V. A Constructive Moral from Spinoza

These achievements, charting as they do his plan of salvation, together constitute his cure for scepticism. We may summarize them under three heads. First, he achieved a unified world, a single substance, whose attributes or modes constitute all that we know. Our senses present us with a variegated and pluralistic set of worlds, but the drift of the mind is surely toward monism. Descartes never achieved it, or achieved it too easily to be of enduring worth. Spinoza tackled heroically the problem, and came out to his own satisfaction with a single world that held together through thick and thin. Its existence as unitary and ideal he validated by the very idea we have of such a world. The manner of his proof has allied him with the famous metaphysicians. The matter of his proof has endeared him to many of the greatest poets these three hundred years. For it was primarily, I suppose, this picture of a unified world, held together in a seamless whole like a wondrous work of art, that made Spinoza *the* philosopher to Lessing, to Goethe, to Herder, to Coleridge, to Shelley, to Santayana. For the logician, alas, there may still be seams in Spinoza's totality, but to the aesthetic

93

eye his universe holds together like a thing of final perfection.

Second, he achieved a divinity for such as no longer believed in God. I have spoken already of Einstein's devotion to this conception. Spinoza's deity has had a peculiar appeal for the scientific-minded. Huxley once declared that ' The student of nature, if his work has not been barren of the best fruit, will have the sense to see that God so conceived is one that only a great fool would deny even in his heart.' Huxley responded, no doubt, not to the ontological basis of proof, but to the identification of nature and deity.

The sun, the moon, the stars, the seas, the hills and the
  plains —
Are not these, O Soul, the very being of Him who reigns?

No scientist is likely to deny a deity who is, as Rabbi Freehof says of Spinoza's, ' Invincible Necessity and Changeless Law.' This attribution of divinity to nature added some comfort if not color to Spinoza's otherwise austere conception of the world. As ' the intellectual love towards God is the very love with which God loves himself,' so also is it the love by which we love ourselves as parts of the whole of nature which God is.

This suggests the third achievement, which completes Spinoza's escape from external assaults and internal scepticism. It is a discovery that we shall further commemorate in both Hume (Chapter IV) and Holmes (Chapter VI), the neutralization of emotions through accommodation to fate. If we cannot get what we want, we may at least learn to want what we get. We might at long last, indeed, learn to want wanting itself. Of Spinoza do Millay's lines ring most poignantly true —

> I gnawed at every root.
> I ate of every plant.
> I came upon no fruit
> So wonderful as want.

Now Spinoza distinguishes sharply between actions, what we do, and passions, what is done to us. Whereas passions may be either good or bad, all actions are always good. What we need therefore, in order to guarantee ourselves against the onslaughts of the world and thus assure perfection to ourselves is that we should always draw first, never allowing the universe to get the drop on us. What we actively accept is not inflicted upon us, but is our own doing and is therefore and thereby good.

Understanding becomes thus our defense against all enslavement of grief and pain; for ' An emotion which is a passion ceases to be a passion as soon as we form a clear and distinct idea of it.' Knowing this, ' we shall,' says Spinoza, ' bear with equanimity those things which happen to us contrary to that which a regard for our advantage postulates. . . . If we understand this clearly and distinctly, that part of us which is called our understanding

. . . will acquiesce in this entirely. . . . For in so far as we understand, we can desire nothing save that which is necessary. . . and therefore . . . the endeavor of the best part of us agrees with the order of the whole of nature.' What is true of us is true also of God, only he, being Nature, does not have so hard a time keeping the jump on that raw Dame. For man acquiescence is difficult, and active acceptance more difficult.

That this independence from the world through active mind is difficult is, however, not the important thing. ' All excellent things are as difficult as they are rare.' The really important thing is that such salvation is possible for mortal man. If Spinoza's God-idea is primarily for scientists, as Rabbi Freehof declares and as numerous cases illustrate, then we may also grant the learned Rabbi that Spinoza's ethics is primarily for ' saints.' But secular saints as children of science still survive, and their minds to them their kingdoms are. The open-minded fixation of their emotions upon the flux of phenomena itself becomes for them a way of life which in truth is the closest approach of our time to the religion of Spinoza.

Weaving these three achievements as warp into our earlier picture of his biography as woof, we may close our positive moral by saying that since Spinoza could not base his own personality upon a social order that he did not feel, he built upon a physical order that had no feeling. He set himself to match the infinite apathy of the cosmos by mastering his own feelings through the power of reason. His central moral conviction is the relativity of all value to individual emotion. The universe, which is God, has no divine compassion, nor any feeling whatever, nor any value at all; we invest it with whatever we feel. But we give all and get nothing; indeed it is a mark of the celebrated intellectual love of God, as Spinoza conceives it, that it does not expect God to love in return. Not out there in the world, no, not even though we pursue it to infinity, is meaning or value to be found; but back here, here in the human mind itself, is all that is worthful. 'We do not desire a thing because we judge it to be good, but, on the contrary, we call that good which we desire.'

If the world condemns us to an attic for habitat and to correspondence for friendship, then in our reverie we build a world as cold as an attic and invest it with values as thin as friendship through correspondence. In saying so, I judge not Spinoza so much as the world. Bare understanding of that world remained for Spinoza, however, and it constituted the heart of his values and the means of his personal salvation, for it subdued the emotions in their vain searching for answering warmth and color that were not there. Such is the etiology of pure intellectuality and such the resulting peace, even if poverty, of spirit.

Austere but active acceptance was the trick of

life whose mastery thus spelled for Spinoza victory over fate. He rediscovered for himself, in short, how to make the best of reality at its worst. Now this is an immortal discovery, always meriting rediscovery in a world that some of the time for all of us and all of the time for some of us permits little alternative to the worst. All honor, then, to Spinoza for distilling the very essence of Stoicism and Christianity into such high personal compensation for the sterility of cosmic neutrality, i.e., *an emotional appreciation of understanding itself*. Whoever can feed thus, with Spinoza, upon himself, when other provender fails, can never wholly starve, though the day of life be long and the diet always meagre.

VI. A NEGATIVE MORAL UNDER THE NEW DEAL

This type of defense against life, commendable as it is when it must be withdrawal or worse, is not very useful when we need to attack rather than to defend. Our contemporary opportunity, bad as it may appear just now, is not yet permanently reduced to making the best out of the worst. We may still reasonably hope to make the worst less bad and the less bad better. The tendency in some quarters to exploit Spinoza as a political guide for the present leaves me uneasy, though I joy to honor him where I think him wise. It leaves me doubly uneasy, however, when reverence for Spinoza is made to ornament a definite modern escapism. I refer to the tendency to mythologize physics with mystic aureoles, to romanticize medievalism in morals under the guise of good taste founded on uncriticized tradition, to realize Platonism by glorifying contemporary dictators, black, red, or brown, as the long sought philosopher kings. I refer, in a word, to the rationalized romanticism of those among us who would purge the social sciences, our best hope of improvement as definition was Spinoza's best bet — purge them, I say, of every element that makes them social and then present science as pure logic to be got at dialectically rather than experimentally. Such attitudes are defeatist, and while they find in Spinoza, and Plato, logical prototypes, they wrong the noble dead by accommodating them to a logic of events, more pregnant than was their ancient logic of discourse.

With reference to our own social problem and a fruitful attitude toward it, I am indeed convinced that Spinoza is a splendid example of the way not to do it. Passing among us as a political realist because he built his system on power, Spinoza actually romanticized the distribution of power which prevailed at his time and place. The trouble is that power itself is not given to men in a sacred lump with implied anathemas against any who would increase or reallocate it. It waxes and wanes in quantity and migrates here and there in habitat. Our task is, as Spinoza truly said, to understand power, its nature and incidence — not however in order to achieve blessedness under the worst distribution of it but in order, if possible, to facilitate a more blessed redistribution of power. Spinoza is not our logical leader in the effort through science to increase power; for though engaged in what for his time was a scientific profession — lens grinding — he elected to seek personal salvation through discovering and contemplating the whole of things rather than social amelioration by detailed mastery of parts. There was a perfectly good reason for this, as we have seen, but it is a reason which makes him unavailable as our political guide today. His logic was introspective and compulsative rather than investigative and creative.

Nor is Spinoza our logical leader in the task of distributing power more justly to all men; for he could not get along with men well enough to understand, much less to improve, the forms of social relations. Not wholly in his stars but partially also in himself must have lain the cause of his lifelong isolation. His last name means ' thorny,' as Rabbi Browne suggests. He could, it appears, be rather difficult in dealing with competitors. No, Spinoza's contribution lay in neither of these fields. It is true that his spirited defense of freedom of thought and speech touched an indispensable element in both the increase and the redistribution of power. It is true also that Spinoza emphasized activity rather than passivity, but this after reducing activity to the kind that goes on in one's head. So much indeed did he emphasize head-action that he romantically rendered the real in terms of clear and distinct ideas.

Now this identification of reality with the clearly conceivable — a practice whose maxim Nietzsche thought ought to be put up as the legend on the portals of every insane asylum — may be all right in theology. But in social philosophy it is the final apotheosis of the status quo; for nothing else can ever appear quite so natural, quite so clear and distinct, as what has become customary. And therefore Spinoza's already indicated disinclination to change inherited political forms or to work out the theory of shifting the incidence of power. The more we prize his escape mechanism, when escape was the only hope, the less are we inclined to recommend him to contemporaries as a social and political guide.

For it is not now too soon to get clear that what society needs is not some romantic escape down paths marked ' personal salvation,' however alluring these paths may be. *What we most need are actual methods for the pooling of insight, genuine social inventions for the sharing of power.* In all probability ignorance of means is a far greater hindrance to social and political amelioration than any lack of noble ends or than is ill will among men. *Concrete inventiveness in the social field* — this is our greatest need. And this can be supplied only by specialists, not specialists in logic, however, not in mathematics, not in any kind of abstractions, but specialists in social relations themselves. One who does not live with men, whatever the reason (and Spinoza had the best), and does not get along with men, whosesoever the fault, cannot reasonably be expected to invent fertile social compromises. Lovers of men who are also fecund of ideas are here our hope.

Those who, like Spinoza, flee men for ideas are not likely to use their ideas, however brilliant they may be, for the discouragingly modest task of elaborating better forms of cooperation in political and social life. Nor are they likely to furnish ideas that can be so used by others. Their ideas will be too good, too clear, for social need.

This sounds paradoxical, I acknowledge, if not actually perverse; but the notion will bear inspection that crystal-clear ideas, instead of directing remedial action, substitute for action. To see things, as Spinoza prescribes, *sub specie aeternitatis,* does allay the emotions, but by inhibiting motion. It does beget repose, but it does so by obscuring just the details necessary as cues for fruitful action. Emerson describes the point of view in his *Brahma:*

> Far and forgot to me are near;
>   Shadow and sunlight are the same;
> The vanished gods to me appear;
>   And one to me are shame and fame.

But, see, from that point of view ' shame and fame ' are one.

To achieve mental clarity and emotional calm by distance from, and so by innocence of, facts is the way to resignation as the price of peace. If that's what we want, then that's the way to get it. Sometimes it's that or worse. It probably was just so for Spinoza. But to take the point of view when it is not necessitated by the logic of events is defeatist, if not discreditable. Let no one think that the procedure is exhausted by other-worldly religions; nor by philosophers who, like Spinoza, must compensate for personal disappointments.

The procedure is at once the glory and the vanity of all abstract science, as Ortega so well declares in his *The Revolt of the Masses.* ' Abstract things,' says he, ' are always clear. So that the clarity of science is not so much in the heads of scientists as in the matters of which they speak. . . . The majority of men of science have given themselves to science through fear of facing life. They are not clear heads; hence their notorious ineptitude in the presence of any concrete situation.' One could document this judgment of Ortega's the more thrillingly, the closer he brought hard-boiled natural scientists before situations that involve social prejudices. Ortega continues: ' Politics is much more of a reality than science, because it is made up of unique situations in which a man suddenly finds himself submerged whether he will or no. Hence it is a test which allows us better to distinguish who are the clear heads and who are the routineers.'

Now, I am convinced that Ortega is right in this, though not in every, provocative conclusion. Next to the vice of complicating the simple is the vice of over-simplifying the complex. How much clearer ideas can be than the things of which they are ideas and yet prove fruitful for dealing with the things, is an open question. But that there is a limit where clarity yields diminishing social returns can be demonstrated by a visit to any insane asylum. The best insurance a devotee of logic can get against going there to live is to go there occasionally to visit.

Among abstract thinkers only such as have something like a sense of humor can in person fulfil the hope raised by the glitter of abstract ideals in the social field. But let us return to Spinoza. A sense of humor, ah yes — a little phrase and quickly spoken; but Spinoza was a belated prophet, without honor in his own country, and prophets specialize in piety, not in humor. He was the last of the medievalists before he was the first of the moderns. A sense of humor, ah yes; but starvation, physical and spiritual, is not the food upon which a sense of humor doth mostly feed. A sense of humor, ah yes; but it has taken three centuries from Spinoza, the serious, to produce Santayana, a disciple mirthful enough to see that if we smile at God, Nature, who created us ' by smiling in her dreams,' drops the mask of indifference which alone Spinoza saw and smiles back at us with engaging candor.

Himself indeed Spinoza saved, but society he could not and cannot save. Pending our discussion of Justice Holmes, whom we have selected to show us the path through doubt to democracy, we can pay Spinoza no safer honor than, borrowing from Plato, to take Spinoza the social thinker, as he did not take himself, with a sense of humor. But our smile at this ' God-intoxicated ' immortal will be more just and more enduring if we remember that while, subject to many factors, a man may or may not live with other men, every man must live with himself. Spinoza discovered how to live uncomplainingly with himself. That is what it means to make the best of life at its worst. Spinoza doubted himself through misery to personal peace.

CHAPTER IV

DOUBTING ONE'S WAY TO HONESTY AND SYMPATHY

Being a double-moral from Hume and Schopenhauer

If we think of our progress thus far in creative scepticism as a descent into Avernus, we are in this chapter to reach our destination. We shall indeed, continuing that figure of speech, stand very quickly in the presence of Pluto himself. It is my constant intent, however, to discover to you what light, if any, there may be in doubt, even in the bottomless pit of complete scepticism and of bitter pessimism. These are the lowest reaches of our present descent: complete scepticism being the intellectual bottom and abject pessimism being the emotional bottom. I shall not seek to relate the two any closer than life relates them; and life, contrary perhaps to popular opinion, often gives the one without the other, sometimes the other without the one. David Hume, our deepest sceptic, was for a fact cheerful enough. Arthur Schopenhauer, our bitterest pessimist, with no cheer left save gloom, found reasons enough to live in the con-

templation of certain verities surviving scepticism.
From the doubt of Hume we shall draw the moral
of reassuring honesty; from the pessimism of
Schopenhauer a moral never needed more than
now, one of far-reaching human sympathy.

I. HUME CONFIRMS THE WORST OF PREVIOUS DOUBTS

It was not in resurrecting and making more conclusive the doubts that other men had had of deity
and of the soul that Hume distinguished himself as
arch-apostle of scepticism. His original, world-
shaking doubt lies beyond all this. But just here,
before going on to that, we must note how he did
finish the career of doubt which Descartes began
and stifled, which Locke cautiously advanced,
which Berkeley furthered but by no means finished, which Spinoza turned to his own contentment. Descartes had indeed saved God from
doubt, but too easily. He did place the self on
such stable foundations, however, that neither
Locke nor Berkeley thought it necessary further
to bulwark his assurance of a thinker to explain
thinking, of a doubter to explain doubting. John
Locke did, however, cast doubt enough upon the
existence of matter to leave it described as an ' I-
know-not-what.' Berkeley, as we have seen, finished that line of early modern doubt, but defended, or, more truly it may be said, assumed, a

spiritual substance personalized as souls and presided over by God, who maintained them through his comprescence. Now it was upon this matter of spiritual substance, too easily established by Descartes and too lightly assumed by Locke and Berkeley, that Hume turned his eyes.

He acknowledged that Berkeley had made his case against matter, but did not the same logic apply destructively to mind? If material substance upon analysis crumbles into qualities, pray what becomes of spiritual substance when you stop to think about it? Can you describe what it is except by its qualities, and are these qualities not ideas rather than substance? Is spiritual substance, then, to be treated as a new ' I-know-not-what,' or shall we be as honest regarding mind as Berkeley was regarding matter, and acknowledge simply that as spiritual substance it is but a superstition? Only the qualities, then, whether of ' mind ' or ' matter,' are real; and these qualities are but sensations or ideas, with no *mind* to be *in*, on this side, and no *matter* to be *of*, on that side. In very truth, the man who insists upon talking the superstition of ' matter, matter ' all the while, ought to be bluntly told: ' Never mind! ' And the devotee who will not but cry ' mind, mind,' ought plainly to be answered: ' It's no matter! '

Hume is very explicit in drawing the case against the existence of spiritual substance. He not only draws it out; he even points it; indeed he points it at himself. 'For my part,' says he, 'when I enter most intimately into what I call myself, I always stumble on some particular perception or other, of heat or cold, light or shade, love or hatred, pain or pleasure. I never can catch myself at any time without a perception, and never can observe anything but the perception.' To every claim of another, on whatever ground, that he had discovered a self back of sensations, ideas, or feelings, Hume only honestly replied: 'I am certain there is no such principle in me.' This 'me' to which he cannot but refer is itself, then, 'nothing but a bundle or collection of perceptions, which succeed each other with an inconceivable rapidity, and are in a perpetual flux and movement.' Nor can it escape notice that this complete disavowal of self, undercutting, as it does, all spiritual substance whatsoever, leaves so-called external objects quite as fitful as they appeared in Berkeley before God was brought to their stabilization. As Hume puts it, 'If colours, sounds, tastes, and smells be merely perceptions, nothing we can conceive is possessed of a real, continued, and independent existence.'

But all this could create little wonder in one who had followed the development of modern philosophy, whether historically from Descartes to Hume, or psychologically as the argument develops in any mind that gets to thinking about the proof of matter and mind. It took honesty to avow the conclusion regarding souls to which the whole argument seemed to point. Locke was far from seeing it. Berkeley was very close to seeing it, but far from avowing it. There is a kind of prideful honesty required of a churchman, or, I suppose, for that matter, of any and every professional man, which tends to hold the welfare of parishioners, or patients, or clients, or even students, more important than any truth that might affect them adversely. Such specialized honesty is, however, but another name for what, if seen from outside the profession, may as appropriately be called by a much less honorific phrase. Now Berkeley is not to be blamed over-much for a vice so common as to pass for professional virtue; but Hume is certainly to be praised the more for having a virtue so lacking in general as to become rare and great in the having, the virtue of seeing things truly and declaring to be true what he saw to be true.

Truth to tell, it was a virtue that literally arose in part from his having no profession. But his failure to have a real profession was in turn due to his own insistence upon following his career-line where it led him, just as he followed the argument of Berkeley to a conclusion adverse to both souls and God. His family had desired him to follow his deceased father's footsteps into the law, had even insisted upon his doing it. But he could not, after a long fair trial, stomach the profession.

Speaking briefly of the whole conflict over the matter, Hume says: ' My studious disposition, my sobriety, and my industry gave my family a notion that the law was a proper profession for me: but I found an insurmountable aversion to everything but the pursuits of philosophy and general learning.' After the trial at law and a shorter fling at business, Hume retired to France on a pittance at twenty-three years of age and composed before he had rounded twenty-five what many believe the greatest philosophical work in English, what all admit one of the great books of all time, his *Treatise of Human Nature*.

II. HUME INSTIGATES AN EARTHQUAKE OF DOUBT

If this volume, which Hume brought back from France with him at twenty-six, could have been measured by the price it brought — fifty pounds — it would not have much disturbed the world. Even if it had stopped at confirming the worst doubts of Descartes and Berkeley, bad as those were when taken together, it might have only mildly shocked the world. For Hume himself readily enough admits that it is impossible *consistently to persevere* in doubt of either matter or mind. But there was something about this *Treatise,* though in 1739 it ' fell dead-born from the press,' that was destined to set Scottish philosophers to work in desperation for a hundred years, rebuilding a shattered structure of faith. There was something about it that was destined to waken the slumbering giant of Germany, Immanuel Kant, from what he called 'a dogmatic slumber.' And with Kant roused and striding, the world was to have no more philosophical peace for a very long time.

That something was primarily Hume's notion of what cause and effect mean, his doubt of the principle of causation. The notion of cause had become the central reliance of the new science, in which Descartes had played his influential rôle. Even yet the opinion is general that science is simply the study of causation, relating all things as cause and effects. Well, to put it somewhat baldly, Hume ruined causation, by stacking so much doubt around its 'necessity' as to reduce it to a feeling of expectation. God lost, not all is lost; souls lost, men have improvised substitutes. But causality lost, where now does man go and how does he go? For you see, my reader, if you look at the matter simply, causation may be considered either a relation between things or forces outside the mind, or a relation between something in and something outside the mind, or merely a relation between things in the mind. Now more disturbing than the fact that Hume left neither mind nor world, is the fact that even if we assume both a mind and a world, Hume left us no way of getting from the one to the other in any dependable fashion. Hume's cogency indeed forced Kant to count causality an invention of the mind superimposed upon its own experiences. Hume cannot make even that much of causality. Things just happen together or apart, like or different, and the mind, passive-like, can expect, though it can give no real reason for the expectation, that things will keep on happening as they have happened. That's cause: constancy of expectation.

You will see that Hume himself constantly talks as though there is a mind and as though there is a world of material things out beyond the mind. He is amazingly frank about it all, even about his own inconsistency, as we shall presently see. You simply cannot talk without talking as though these things were so, whether they are or not. Now Hume is fully convinced that every proof that they are so falls completely down, and yet he is simply like the rest of us, caught in a predicament of having, in order to talk at all, to talk contrary to fact. All this explanation, so that you may not be troubled about certain inconsistencies in his statement of the case. If it is now, or ever is, your good fortune to read Hume through, you'll discover that he sees around himself much better than either you or I do, and is yet honest enough to blink no difficulties, not even his inconsistencies of speech.

Talking as though he had a mind and that mind a world, Hume puts very simply his conclusions regarding causation. ' All our reasoning concerning causes and effects,' says he, ' are derived from nothing but custom; and . . . belief is more properly an act of the sensitive, than of the cogitative part of our natures.' We cannot, of course, speak with precision of one object's causing another, since we can know nothing whatsoever of objects independent of their qualities. Nor are we in any better way of asserting relations between what is ' in ' the mind and what is ' outside ' the mind, since even if we knew anything about ' mind ' in which one is, we certainly know nothing whatsoever about what is outside the mind. All that causation can really mean, then, is a relation between ideas. But there is obviously no necessary connection between these, since there is no proved outside world to necessitate the connection and no mind behind ideas to ground a necessity of connection. The only relations that are left are those between ideas flowing along in the stream of sensations, which stream we merely call our ' minds.'

These floating qualities have only chance associations, as it were, and so no necessary relations. The full force of this will be little missed by divorcing it now from the radical scepticism of both self and the world. Let us say, against whatever background you yourself may have, that it is habit which determines the connection of all things that you know. This does not miss Hume's own belief very far. You think, for instance, that the sun will rise tomorrow. Ordinarily you'd say that you *know* that it will rise tomorrow. The only knowledge in this case is expectation based upon habit formed from past experience. It is the same kind of ' knowledge ' that the turkey has — if any — when on the basis of experience he runs to his mistress to get fed, and gets it in the neck instead. It is only in legend that he warns himself with a premonitory soliloquy:

> Dey's a cu'ious kin' o' shivah
>   runnin' up an' down my back,
> An' I feel my feddahs rufflin'
>   all de day,
> An' my laigs commence to trimble
>   evah blessid step I mek;
> W'en I sees a ax, I tu'ns my
>   head away.

Now it does not take much discussion to make our predicament as dire as that of the turkey around Thanksgiving time, unless we can depend upon causation. Not only is this serious for our common life; it is equally serious for science. If false, the view is difficult to refute; if true, it is disastrous to any certainty, in science or life. Indeed, it is not difficult to imagine and crave feelings more pleasant than those that arise in us when we must confront a universe as whimsical as Hume's thrust at causation leaves this universe. This, then, is what Hume did after he really got going: he destroyed the possibility of any certain knowledge, even if we could recover God, the soul, and the external world of matter. No wonder it shook Kant from slumber; dogmatists more dogmatic than Kant have been staggered by Hume ever since. I dare say that you yourself, my dear reader, feel none too certain of yourself right this minute. Well, that is perhaps Hume's worst; but, something, if less shocking, still more intimate, remains as Hume's final gift to you.

III. Hume Does not Spare even our Moral Verities

Complete as Hume's scepticism is in the fields already traversed, his treatment of morality, to which we now pass, is not soon to be forgotten. As is his habit, he goes at once to the heart of the matter. In a passage fully deserving all the fame it has received, Hume declares: ' In every system of morality which I have hitherto met with, I have always remarked that the author proceeds for some time in the ordinary way of reasoning, and establishes the being of a God, or makes observations concerning human affairs; when of a sudden I am surprised to find that instead of the usual copulations of propositions, *is,* and *is not,* I meet with no proposition that is not connected with an *ought,* or an *ought not.'* Marveling, as many sensitive souls have both before and since, at the audacity displayed by moral mentors who without hesitancy declare of others, ' You ought to do this or that,' Hume thinks that dictation ought surely to rest on extraordinarily firm foundations. It is bad enough for a scrupulous mind to out-talk its information as to facts. It is much worse to exhibit impudence with reference to conduct. Hume, therefore, puts to morality a great question not unlike the one he put to science. To science he said: ' How come *causation?* ' To morality he said: ' How come *duty?* '

This slipping from the field of facts, where we say ' is ' and ' is not,' into another field, where we order others or command ourselves with ' ought ' and ' ought not,' though usually done as Hume says ' imperceptibly,' is nevertheless, as he observes, ' of the last consequence.' Hume examines the matter as critically as he has examined the matters already discussed. The upshot of his examination is that just as causation is dissipated into habits, so morality appears to be born of feeling and to function as convenience. ' Morality,' as Hume says, ' is more properly felt than judged of.' If Hume's general conclusion in morals, ' Reason is, and ought only to be, the slave of the passions,' finds us better prepared than his reduction of causality to custom in the field of science, it is a tribute to the influence already exerted by his and similar doctrines upon the laws, customs, and theories that have gone into our education. We had, however, best not let familiarity minimize the importance of his views in the moral field, whether they be true or false.

To say, indeed, that there's neither right nor wrong but feeling makes it so, is tremendously important if true; and perhaps even more important if false. Particularly is it important when taken, as Hume takes it, into the field of practice, and used as determiner of justice and injustice. Just as there can be no action ' virtuous, or morally good, unless there be in human nature some motive to produce it distinct from the sense of its morality,' so there can be nothing just save what is useful and nothing unjust save what is harmful. ' Justice is an artificial, and not a natural virtue.'

This has, of course, become in America our utilitarian view of law and justice, a fact due no little to Hume's influence. Bentham, to whom with James and John Stuart Mill, we trace much of our philosophy of law and political action, regarded Hume as his master, so far as Hume went. ' No sooner had I read,' says Bentham of the appropriate part of Hume's *Treatise*, ' than I felt as if scales had fallen from my eyes. . . . That the foundations of all *virtue* are laid in *utility*, is there demonstrated.' Remarking that ' self-interest is the original motive to the stablishment of justice,' Hume indeed goes on to explain the origin of society itself as an effort on the part of man to remove his three greatest inconveniences: ' By the conjunction of forces, our power is augmented: by

the partition of employments, our ability in-
creases: and by mutual succor we are less exposed
to fortune and accidents. 'Tis by this additional
force, stability, and *security,* that society becomes
advantageous.'

This, to be sure, is not the whole of Hume's
teaching upon justice or morals. We can only exhibit the main drift here, as elsewhere. And his
main drift in morals is, first, to undermine any
authoritative claim of duty in the name of conscience or religion; second, to reduce moral claims
to feelings; and, third, to judge such feelings in
the light of individual pleasures and pains that attend and follow to constitute their social utility
and disutility. On any final and absolute Right
or Duty, Hume is negative. Individual feelings
and estimates of pleasures and pains, these are
the humble stuff of Hume's ethics. Social convenience and inconvenience, these are the determina-
ble stuff of law and order.

IV. HONESTY AS THE PRECIPITATE OF HUME'S
DOUBT

In turning to the moral derivable from Hume's
scepticism, I do not engage myself, here any more
than elsewhere, to show you that this sceptic created something to take the place of everything he
destroyed. To try to do this would indeed be for
me to deny by my example the one great virtue to

which I wish to point as the moral from Hume — honesty. I do not even know, nor shall I try to prove, that Hume's honesty is a consequence of his scepticism. But it did attend his doubt, and it does illustrate the truth that doubt, even when extreme, is compatible with intellectual and moral integrity.

Hume for a fact did, as we have so lately seen, put something in the place of the authoritative morality which he undermined: he put a democratic ethics, in theory at least, so that every man who feels pleasure and suffers pain must be reckoned with by those who wish conveniently to keep on sitting in places of power. It remained for the other utilitarians after Hume to detail the principle into the political maxim that, in casting up final accounts for happiness, ' each one should count for one and nobody for more than one.' But the theory of this democratic ethics is all in Hume, straight and clear. He made very evident also that even though justice be an ' artificial virtue,' artificial virtue that prevails is to be preferred to ' natural ' or ' divine ' justice that makes no pleasurable adjustment of human pains.

Our sceptic did not, however, restore the selves which he had doubted away, or the matter lost in the limbo of superstition, or the deity gently left in the quietude of nescience. It is true that he seems, as he said, to have left religion where he found it; it is true that, though he could find no 'soul' in himself, he continued to use terms like '*me,*' '*mine,*' and '*I*'; and it is also true that, though material substance had no place in his logic, he continued to utilize notions of objects external to himself, as though the world of common sense still stood intact. Apart from mere inconsistencies in the use of language, which as we have said are to an extent inevitable for all of us who talk, Hume, for a fact, had deeper inconsistencies with reference to most of the major subjects discussed in the *Treatise*.

It is, in truth, just here that we find our major moral. Hume had an intellectual humility which if it be not honesty at its highest, alone makes the highest honesty possible. Not all men, by any means, know when they are out-talking their information; and far fewer than know it will, caught in a pinch, acknowledge it. Hume nearly always knew; and when he knew, he acknowledged. Without this personal character even the possession of truth is dangerous; and with it doubt is denatured of all save its cleansing value. I do not mean that Hume did not sometimes, especially with reference to religion, publish perhaps less than he thought to be the truth. But what he did publish as true could be trusted implicitly, for he goes perhaps as far as the human mind can in claiming only what he saw and claiming it only as he saw it. At the close of Book I of the *Treatise*, for instance, lest he might from universal human frailty have slipped unconsciously somewhere into such phrases as ' it is evident,' ' it is certain,' ' it is undeniable,' he enters a ' caveat ' to his readers against even himself, begging them to know that any such slips, if detected, ' imply no dogmatical spirit, nor conceited idea of my own judgment, which are sentiments that I am sensible can become nobody, and a sceptic still less than any other.'

But this is only the form of his great virtue. Its intimate contents further enhance it. ' Doubts stole in, dissipated, returned,' he wrote a friend of his early growth, ' were again dissipated, returned again; and it was a perpetual struggle of a restless imagination against inclination, perhaps against reason.' Now this kind of experience is no more than we have seen Descartes and Berkeley, almost even Anselm, confess. But the very act of confessing doubt usually carries such a penumbra of pride as implies either that the doubt has been cured before the confession or that he who doubts it not, argues himself beyond the pale of respect. Hume has a virtue here that no other doubter that we have discussed has illustrated.

He acknowledges doubts or beliefs that land him in contradictions, and thus amount to confessions of impotence not easily, if at all, harmonizable with pride. Let me make very clear what I mean. Near the close of Part I, for instance, he declares after a line of reasoning that makes the declaration more than a dramatic gesture: 'We have therefore no choice left, but betwixt a false reason and none at all. For my part, I know not what ought to be done in the present case.' And at the end of Part II, reviewing what he had said upon the important matter of whether one is always one and the same person, Hume acknowledges: ' I must confess, I neither know how to correct my former opinions, nor how to render them consistent. . . . I cannot discover any theory which gives me satisfaction on this head. . . . In short, there are two principles which I cannot render consistent, nor is it in my power to renounce either of them.' Now, my reader, if you be still there, I want to tell you that I think I know how rare this species of honesty is among men of the world. I wonder if you realize how rare it is among philosophers? In my opinion it is as fine as it is rare.

Its fruit is not only the extraordinary charity Hume shows for the opinions of others, but the even more remarkable tolerance he shows toward moods in himself, which though different, even contradictory, are yet each authentic. This kind of tolerance at home is even rarer, if possible, than that kind of charity abroad. I am well aware that the reader may frown at, rather than approve, the direction of my thought upon this matter. But I hold that in a specialized age a divided self, within reason and outside the asylum, is bad only in being thought bad. Hume illustrates my thought, whether the reader can agree with me in approving Hume or not. After describing a sceptical mood in which he is ' ready to reject all belief and reasoning, and can look upon no opinion even as more probable or likely than another,' Hume announces in a famous passage: ' I dine, I play a game of backgammon, I converse, and am merry with my friends.'

Now, in such a gay mood, as Hume goes on to remark, it is easy to despise scepticism and resolve never to indulge such mood again. Such impetuosity, however, would be more heroic than wise. For other times will bring other moods with their legitimate claims upon one: ' I am tired with amusement and company, and have indulged a *reverie* in my chamber, or in a solitary walk by a river side, I feel my mind all collected within itself, and am naturally *inclined* to carry my view into all those subjects, about which I have met with so many disputes in the course of my reading and conversation.' In such a converse mood, it is easy to despise frivolity, and once and all to forswear it. Such impetuosity, however, would be more heroic than wise. Now Hume not only indulges these radical alternations of moods — we all do that — but he acknowledges the practice, and even justifies it. Moreover, his justification is not of the ambiguous type that purports to assimilate either to the other or to show that either enriches or enhances the other. That is, he does not give a *good*, but the *real*, reason for his action. He does each because then and there he wants to do just that.

In short he illustrates the type of self-honesty which declares good what is actually found in experience to be good, and has as a result of his pains in doing so a preoccupation to fit every major mood. He seems to say: Let the night justify nocturnal doings and the day its own shifts; sufficient unto each is the good thereof. And then he climaxes the rich discussion of this (to us) somewhat ticklish matter of the divided self, with this inimitable gem: ' A true sceptic will be diffident of his philosophical doubts, as well as of his philosophical convictions; and will never refuse any innocent satisfaction which offers itself, upon account of either of them.' David Hume, may thy equable tribe on earth increase!

These several precipitates of Hume's character, if not of his scepticism, I have called honesty, and have recommended them to you as fruits from, if not of, doubt. There remains one last ornament of Hume's way of life. His character illustrates it even better than his words declare it. It is the pure principle of intellectual honesty, the truth that knowing the truth is more important than the truth known, that telling the truth is more important than the truth that is told. This is an insight which, did men know it and exemplify it, would lift heavy responsibilities from tired shoulders, i.e., the worry of deciding what truth is safe to know and teach. The contribution of Hume's words upon the matter is that there is in the very fact and the inevitability of truth, catharsis for the grief it bears and spreads. The contribution of his life is that, having lost more than most in the quest for truth — lost certainty of his own soul, lost God, lost the world — he nevertheless lived happily and died nobly. Look at his words; they explain his life: ' Nothing is more certain than that despair has almost the same effect upon us with enjoyment, and that we are no sooner acquainted with the impossibility of satisfying any desire than the desire itself vanishes. When we see that we have arrived at the utmost extent of human reason, we sit down contented.' No deeper or better words have been uttered by modern mind than those. Spinoza, too, knew this wisdom, knew it and lived it.

Look at Hume's life; it nobly fulfils those wise words. His own opinion of his character is well attested by those who journeyed with him in life and by those who stood by him in death. Of himself he says: ' I was a man of mild dispositions, of command of temper, of an open, social, and cheerful humour, capable of attachment, but little susceptible of enmity, and of a great moderation in all my passions.' Of his life, Adam Smith says: ' His temper, indeed, seemed to be more happily balanced, if I may be allowed such an expression, than that of any other man I have ever known. . . . Upon the whole, I have always considered him, both in his lifetime, and since his death, as approaching as nearly to the idea of a perfectly wise and virtuous man, as perhaps the nature of human frailty will permit.' Of his death, the attending physician, Dr. Black, writes Adam Smith: ' He continued to the last perfectly sensible, and free from much pain or feeling of distress. He never dropped the smallest expression of impatience; but when he had occasion to speak to the people about him, always did it with affection and tenderness. . . . He died in such a happy composure of mind, that nothing could exceed it.'

Such was, so lived, thus died David Hume, the most sceptical mind of modern times.

V. From Hume's Affirmation to Schopenhauer's Negation of the 'Will to Live'

Hume died naturally in bed, and, as we have seen, even happily. But with the will to fit an act to every mood, which we have also remarked in him, Hume wrote a defense, published posthumously, of those who died wherever and howsoever they themselves decided. His defense of suicide was only one of the links with Schopenhauer, who also defended suicide while strongly advising against it on grounds that we shall presently explore. Suffice it now to say that Hume's defense arose out of a love for life, Schopenhauer's out of distrust of life. Hume would admit men to die, upon occasion, to keep them from dishonoring life with hopeless pain or preventable shame; Schopenhauer would caution men, who justly preferred death, to go on living to spite life, to circumvent the very will to live. Hume was a happy sceptic; Schopenhauer was a sceptical pessimist.

But the latter's scepticism is relatively unimportant in his philosophy of life. It was what he knew that he felt rather than what he felt that he didn't know that troubled Schopenhauer. Since we have let Hume represent, as he naturally does, our extreme of scepticism, we shall pass lightly over the sceptical aspects of Schopenhauer's philosophy in order to concentrate upon what he himself emphasizes, the deep, vast evils of life —

> His wit all see-saw, between that pain and this,
> Now high, now low, now master up, now miss,
> And he himself one vile Antithesis
> To any show of joy, to every hint of bliss.

There is little in Schopenhauer's life that is beautiful; but his doctrine does eventuate in a sort of consolation of desolation. Upon this we shall wish to meditate; we may indeed find something in it to celebrate as a final fruit for pessimism.

First, however, a brief glance at Schopenhauer's scepticism. Arising from and breathing in a vastly different climate of opinion from that of Hume, which we have so recently quitted, Schopenhauer distinguished two major aspects of the world about us. The title of his celebrated book shows what these aspects are: *The World as Will and as Idea.* Kant, after Hume, had taken into the mind all that is really knowable, sensations from unknown outside sources being the content for such forms as space and time and such relations as cause-effect furnished by the mind itself. All this Schopenhauer believed. All that we can know about the world is veritably idea, and there is no need to assume that there is any more than that to the objective world. ' All that exists,' as Schopenhauer has it, ' exists only for the subject ' — that is, all that exists *save* the subject itself. There is, however, as we have remarked in Chapter I, a very general reluctance on the part of thinkers to follow even their own logic into solipsism. Schopenhauer not only sees this, he exploits it. ' The inward reluctance with which any one accepts the world as merely his idea,' he clearly discerns, ' warns him that this view of it, however true it may be, is nevertheless one-sided.' And though, as Schopenhauer goes on to declare, ' it is a conception from which he can never free himself,' it is nevertheless ' adopted in consequence of some arbitrary abstraction.'

This arbitrary abstraction results from not attaching as much importance to the subject as is attached to ideas as objects. The subject *has* ideas; but it *is* will. The world falls, thus, into two parts, objects always and only known; subjects always knowing, but never known. ' As the world is in one aspect entirely *idea,* so in another it is entirely *will.*' ' A reality which is neither,' like Kant's things-in-themselves, as Schopenhauer sees, or like Descartes' matter, as Berkeley and Hume saw, such a reality is, Schopenhauer concludes, ' the phantom of a dream.' Subjects as wills know ideas by feeling, but are themselves never known by or through ideas. The external world is thus crumbled, as by Berkeley, into ideas; but the internal world, the subject, is saved, though without God as in Berkeley — and to how much sadder an end is it saved!

For with the self described as a yearning, striving, passionate will, the process of knowledge, though real enough, is subordinated to that of feeling, which represents the inner nature of the will. The will knows the world, because the world is its own ideas objectified; but it feels itself as the knowing reality, and feels itself as hopelessly bad. Schopenhauer is not sceptical, then, of our knowing the objectified order, for there are no real objects to know save our ideas. But, worse than ordinary scepticism, he knows that what is underneath ideas to be known is not *worth* the knowing. ' That our existence itself implies a fault is proved by death.'

VI. The Grounds of Schopenhauer's Pessimism

Now, where did Schopenhauer get so mordant a picture of reality as will? What nerved him so insistently to the glum query

> . . . How arrives it joy lies slain,
> And why unblooms the best hope ever sown?

Where, my reader, does any man get his picture of life, save out of himself? Do you get yours otherwise, otherwhere? You may easily infer, then, as you read this pessimist's indictment of life that he was not a happy man. Indeed, he neither loved life nor passed it on.

> His father and his mother
> They had a likely son,
> And he has none.

But let us not too easily reduce his philosophy to a biography. To do so raises as many queries as it answers. I hazard the guess that if you are now reading, or shall ever read, his great work through, you will find more of yourself in him than you have yet recognized. Each man writes from *inward,* but he reaches *outward;* and, certainly, the picture of the outward order which Schopenhauer draws from withinward reflects a world that you yourself have skirted, even if with somewhat averted eyes.

131

The spirit of his case for misery can be had from a simple illustration. Take eating. It's a fine sport, if not a great art; an activity very widespread among men and animals, and the source, it is said, of no little pleasure. And yet you get no pleasure out of eating unless you are hungry. Quite the contrary, as you well know. The only pleasure there is to eating is the satisfaction of hunger. But hunger is itself pain — a pain imperceptible at first, then dim and dawning, then eager and watery, until at last ravenous and maddening. But all this takes time, the passing from mere sniffing of suspected food to actual readiness to snatch the first thing you see. Now, the pleasure of eating is the satisfaction, as you agree, of this state called hunger. The satisfaction is seldom, if ever, perfect; and when it is, it is much shorter than the pain caused by the coming on of hunger. A satisfaction that never equalizes the dissatisfaction which alone makes it possible — that's life. Ever repeated so!

But not all of life. That's life *at its best*. This increment of misery from want at its best grows into every sort of hellish gnawing where wants exist for which no satisfaction is provided. And ' for one wish that is satisfied,' Schopenhauer guesses, ' there remain at least ten which are denied.' Moreover, thinks our gloomy one, ' No attained object of desire can give lasting satisfaction, but merely a fleeting gratification; it is like the alms thrown to the beggar, that keep him alive today that his misery may be prolonged till the morrow. Therefore as long as our consciousness is filled by our will, so long as we are given up to the throng of desires with their constant hopes and fears, so long as we are the subject of willing, we can never have lasting happiness nor peace.' Since, however, the subject is doomed by fate to perpetual willing, being naturally constituted so, he is ' thus constantly stretched on the revolving wheel of Ixion, pours water into the sieve of the Danaids, is the ever-longing Tantalus.'

Now that is the authentic picture of life for you, as drawn by Arthur Schopenhauer; drawn, miserable man, with no touch of woman's hand to lighten care, no glance of love to thrill. ' Woman's hand ' —bah! ' When nature slit the human race into two halves,' snorts he, ' she did not make the division quite through the middle . . . that undersized, narrowshouldered, broadhipped, shortlegged sex! ' Spare Schopenhauer ' woman's hand to lighten care! ' But love? Ah, yes, love!

> Winning love we win the risk of losing,
> And losing love is as one's life were riven.

' In the midst of the tumult,' reminisces Schopenhauer, ' straining all powers to satisfy infinite needs and to ward off multifarious sorrows . . . we see the glances of two lovers meet longingly: yet why so secretly, fearfully, and stealthily? Because these lovers are the traitors who seek to perpetuate the whole want and drudgery, which would otherwise speedily reach an end; this they wish to frustrate, as others like them have frustrated it before.'

'What then, misanthrope, misogynist,' I think I hear you readers, especially you feminine readers, ask, 'what of a nice quick dose of suicide, for all your grouchy woes?' Schopenhauer first replies that 'there is no one living perhaps who would not have made an end of his life if this end were something purely negative — a sudden cessation of existence.' But his first reply cannot be his last; for to take one's life is but backhandedly to recognize the will to live as your master. You must conquer the monster, not yield to him.

VII. Schopenhauer's Prescription for Weltschmerz

Not through death can we escape from the will to live, but only through denying life while we live. 'Suicide does not cost . . . persons any self-conquest, they do not require to form any resolution.' Indeed, according to Schopenhauer, 'the suicide wills life, and is only dissatisfied with the conditions under which it has presented itself to him.' Our dissatisfaction must be of sterner stuff than that; it must be turned against life itself. Suicide is too easy to be effective against this enemy of man. We must somehow circumvent the very will to live; failing this, we must mortify it. Ascetic religion is the great aid to its mortification; art and morality our reliances for transcending the will.

As regards religion, Schopenhauer is well known as one of the early voices of Buddhistic insight in the West. He glorified also what he believed to be the major emphasis of Christianity. But beware, my Christian reader, his Christianity is not the modern easy kind. ' Let no one think,' he warns, ' that Christianity it favourable to optimism; for, on the contrary, in the Gospels world and evil are used as almost synonymous.' The true saint, of whatever faith or sort, occupied a high place in Schopenhauer's estimation. For as every sinner has a future, so every saint has had a past; he does not respect the world. Now only he who turns his back upon the world and all it offers can really frustrate the demands of the flesh, can effectively mortify the desires of the spirit. The saint, having done so, has certainly set his face toward Jerusalem. Yes, Jerusalem, he will have it so, in spite of the protest of my Christian reader. ' If Christians knew,' Schopenhauer replies to your protest, ' what Christianity is, they would proclaim me the greatest Christian of the lot, for I affirm at the source — and for the reason which was affirmed in the beginning — that the only way really to live is to die; and to die means to get rid of the will to live itself.' While it is a matter of some pride to Schopenhauer to justify this alliance with Christianity, it is not a matter on which depends his argument. If he were beaten out of Jerusalem, out of heaven, yea out of hell, still Nirvana remains. There all men know, without dispute, lies nescience of individual willing, quiescence for individual consciousness altogether.

> A time there was — as one may guess
> And as, indeed, earth's testimonies tell —
> Before the birth of consciousness,
> When all went well.
>
> .   .   .   .
>
> But the disease of feeling germed,
> And primal rightness took the tinct of wrong;
> Ere nescience shall be reaffirmed
> How long, how long?

Since, however, life cannot be successfully denied by any mere wilful assertion of will-lessness — even the saint must be watchful here — art offers a means of temporarily circumventing the will. Music was Schopenhauer's preference for catharsis, for he saw in it ' the copy of the will itself, whose objectivity the Ideas are.' Since the world as idea is objectified will, the more universal the objectification the more fully can the will lose itself in identity therewith. Every form of art is in some fashion the glinting through the will-soaked particular of the more will-free universal. So in poetry, in painting, and in sculpture can the harassed soul now and then find in absorbed contemplation surcease from its restless striving.

Nor is Nature herself lacking in medicinal virtue. Whatever has beauty holds promise of some relief. ' Nature convulsed by a storm; the sky darkened by black threatening thunder-clouds; stupendous, naked, overhanging cliffs, completely shutting out the view; rushing, foaming torrents, absolute desert; the wail of the wind sweeping through the clefts of the rocks ' — all these, and such as these, offer relief and release to the recreant will. Indeed every form of art or manifestation of nature in proportion as it generates a feeling of the sublime, woos the will toward, if never to, *will-lessness*.

But morality combines, as it were, the relief offered by art and the release found in asceticism. For by morality Schopenhauer understands nothing more or less than sympathy. ' Since all grief,' says he, ' because it is a mortification — a call to resignation — has in it the possibility of rendering one holy, therefore it is that great sorrow — deep pangs — arouse in us a certain reverence for the sufferer; but the sufferer becomes wholly venerable only when, seeing his whole life as one chain of sorrow, he does not yet dwell on the enchainment of circumstances that brought grief to just his life.' What can indeed most influence men ' to good deeds and works of love, is simply the *knowledge of the suffering of others*, which is directly understood from their own suffering and placed on a level with it. But it follows from this that pure love is in its nature sympathy.' Since the will's constant manifestation in men is, and must be, suffering, if we can isolate our doom and fate as the object of a pure self-forgetting contemplation, we seem to achieve all objects in one and at once. ' To become pure subject of knowledge,' as we do in contemplating the objectification of our own suffering wills, ' is to be quit of oneself.' And that is salvation, is blessedness. Sympathy becomes thus the highest morality and the noblest religion. ' All true and pure love,' says Schopenhauer, ' is sympathy, and all love which is not sympathy is selfishness.' This view casts a more tolerable light upon his earlier aspersion upon love. Sexual love it is that is the doorway to further misery, not only of participants but of the pathetic progeny begotten of love's joyous pain. But genuine love, sympathy for suffering and pity for woe, is the final word of any morality in touch with life and the very essence of every religion that centers itself around salvation.

Nor does this solicitude born of suffering spend itself in Schopenhauer exclusively upon human pain. All creation groaneth and travaileth together in the throes of a primeval fault, and nothing that suffers can be alien to the suffering human soul. Animals pay in pain for our poor respite from hunger. Indeed, if I may here introduce the hero of our next chapter, he will make you feel what Schopenhauer meant. ' It is not the pains of the conquering strong,' declares William Pepperell Montague, ' that call for our pity, but rather the pains of the utterly vanquished and crushed. Pains, for example, of small rabbits delivered as playthings to young eagles or fox pups by their mothers to be nibbled, gnawed, or pecked at slowly; toads beneath the harrow, cats beneath the wheels of our cars, or captured mice in the claws of those same cats. For such pains there is no compensating heroism, no high religion or philosophy to snatch victory from defeat — nothing but writhing and screaming, trembling, terror, and despair.'

CHAPTER V

DOUBTING ONE'S WAY TO COURAGE AND ENTHUSIASM

Being a moral from William Pepperell Montague

Having reached the bottom of the pit of doubt, we are from this chapter climbing steadily up. Not that the very bottom was utterly unendurable. Hume taught us better than that, and Schopenhauer lived in spite of woe. We found in Hume's beliefless world some courageous alternation of moods to guide our own unintegrated selves, deep honesty to safeguard the mind's integrity, and cheer enough for a life not too exacting of logical consistency. We found that Schopenhauer predicated on suffering a sympathy that redeemed the suffering itself with the flicker of an eternal flame. All this in spite of the fact that really during the last chapter we were ' hanging on the ropes.' That stage of our fight is over. From here on, beginning in this very chapter, we're ' up and at 'em.' Life is now to seem worth while not in spite of gloom and doubt, but through them if not indeed because of them. We have for our present hero a fine flowering of the modern spirit. William Pepperell

Montague has all the honesty of Hume; he blinks no facts, however adverse they may be to morale. He is as sympathetic as Schopenhauer, heroically hurling the suffering of his and Schopenhauer's mutual canine friend as infamy into the face of " any God who ever lived in heaven if with omnipotence to draw upon he had ordained . . . the puzzled mounting wretchedness of a single dog lost on the streets of a city."

I. Youthful Doubt and How It Flowered

But let us begin at the beginning, even though we cannot follow through to a determinate end the thought of a still living man with an evergrowing mind. We meet in Montague the first living man that we have taken as a model, and the first American. Himself a professor at Columbia University and a man of many parts, he tells delightful stories of his early years that will surely resurrect from the limbo of things long forgotten many of our own childhood doubts and longings. He was early, and always, interested in the soul. His mother had tried to satisfy and quiet his first curiosity by telling him that ' the soul was that which made you laugh and cry and think and move.' He at once puzzled her with the question as to whether, then, ' you could get it out by boring very carefully up through the foot and leg until you reached it somewhere in the chest.' His father, impatiently breaking in at this point, told him that he ' must never think of the soul in that way, that it was not at all the kind of thing that had a place inside the body from which it could be fished out.'

But Montague was not satisfied by either his mother's hesitant or his father's impatient negative. If there is a soul, there must be some way of getting at it. Nor did the New England congregation of his early Sundays, which gave him ' a poignant sense of the beauty of the Christian doctrine,' satisfy him upon this deeper matter, though it did teach him ' love and enthusiasm for one half of the Church, righteous hate and contempt for the other.' Nor yet did his teachers at Harvard — the great Royce, the dashing James, the perfect Palmer, the soaring Santayana, or the worshipful Peirce — ever satisfy him upon the soul; whether it exists, where it exists, how it can be discovered. From college he went out, not to be a lawyer as he had once feared, but gladly to be a philosopher — a philosopher in search of the soul.

He went out into the world indeed with an unusual equipment for an American of the nineties. Bellamy's *Looking Backward* had early made a socialist of him, sensitizing him deeply to all souls and their care. Articles from Madam Blavatsky and other theosophists had fancifully elaborated his early notion of the soul as something that could be got at, an immaterial material thing within us. Numbers always had for him, as for Pythagoras of old, what Montague acknowledges as ' an almost pathological fascination.' Not to regard them as entities in themselves, as something literally ' out there,' seemed to him ' not only false but idiotic.' Out there, they must be: ' more steadfast than the stars and more clear and beautiful than any existing things can ever hope to be.' With such childhood background and such early adult equipment, he went out into the world to be a philosopher, with what he describes as ' the taint of the circle-squarer ' and a willingness ' in philosophy, at least . . . to do everything once.'

And he went to California.

Now what has happened to many a man who went to California happened to Montague, only more so to Montague. He fell in with a band of philosophers, who taught him many, many things. But they did not wean him away from pressing the curiosity which he had voiced at his mother's knee. It is doubtful whether he could have been weaned away from that by even the heroic onslaught suggested by an impious wag, who hearing so often that men learned religion at their mother's knee, proposed to stop the propaganda by cutting off all mothers' knees. Montague had gone West — to California, it was — to find the soul; and no band of philosophers, not even such a resourceful band as he admits that he found there, could stop him.

Then one day Fate overtook this belief-ful doubter, Fate overtook him in California. Mighty events, Carlyle says, hang upon a straw; the crossing of a brook determines the conquest of the world, or, we may now add, the mastery of the soul. Montague saw from a little bridge across a little brook — at Berkeley, in California, it was — he saw, looking down into . . . no, I'll not try to tell you where he was looking or what he saw. I'll only tell you what he said he saw. He saw, or thought he saw, or felt that he thought that he saw, what, he earnestly acknowledges, ' has meant more to me than anything else that has happened in my life.' ' It was,' he continues, ' as if I could look into and down through each point of space and perceive a kind of well of infinite depth. The new realm was like a fourth dimension in that it was perpendicular to the three dimensions of space, and yet as contained within each point it seemed to be a lesser thing than a spacial dimension.'

Is that enough, dear reader, of what Montague saw, or thought he saw, or felt that he thought that he saw at Berkeley in California? No? Then this: ' I described it to myself as a " hypo-space," a realm of negative dimensionality or essential fractions of the punctiform units of an extensive manifold. It seemed to be the domain of intensity and density, so that if I thought of a continuous solid being diminished in its extent until it had shrunk to a point, that would not be a zero of mass magnitude, for each point of a solid must be as different from a point of empty space as a finite sphere of

solid is from the same sphere of empty space.'
Now that's what Montague saw, or thought he saw
— at Berkeley, in California.

But that's by no means all that he thought he
saw. He not only saw things, but you can see for
yourself that he can say things. Now he has five
times as many words as I have quoted, all English
words too, in which he tries to tell more, if not all,
of what he saw. Since I cannot quote all the words,
let me tell you where they are. They are in the
story he tells of his philosophic life, *Contemporary
American Philosophy*, Volume II, pp. 151–152
(edited by Adams and Montague, published by the
Macmillan Company). It is not necessary to quote
all his words here, or for you to see them at all, for
that matter. It is enough for you to know that he
saw things there of the greatest importance, of such
importance that looking back upon that ' daze of
ecstasy ' from the sober vantage of the years, he
can now say, ' my dominant philosophic purpose
has been to make clear to myself and others the full
meaning of what had been revealed in my intuition
while crossing the brook.' This is enough for our
purpose. For our purpose is to exhibit Montague,
our genial friend and present guide, as a fruitful example of the way in which in modern times doubt
turns itself to true, useful, and satisfying ends. I
shall not labor his scepticism, but rather his method
of capitalizing his doubts. He has been a sensitive
child of a sceptical age, bearing in himself most of

the spores of its wonder and confusion. But more than most modern men who honestly doubt, Montague has maintained at white heat a robust will to believe.

II. Doubt Among the Historic Methods

If our intent in this book had been to give a systematic evaluation or even adequate account of scepticism, we should have had to imitate the example set by Montague in his great book, *The Ways of Knowing.* To imitate, however, would be difficult and to surpass more difficult still in this case. Indeed, Montague has there done the systematic job, in both aspects, so well that it did not occur to us to invite comparison by undertaking it. A much more modest thing we have been seeking to do — merely to illustrate typical cases of doubt with emphasis upon their creative aspects. This motive which absolves our effort from comparison with Montague makes quite unnecessary any real effort to parade what he himself has done in the historic field. Let me only say enough about his splendid survey to turn the reader's attention emphatically to that weighty book.

Montague has there sought to treat more or less exhaustively all the ways the human mind has of knowing. Therein is discerned what we have already noted, the positive bent of our author's

mind. He is a sceptic only when life has made
him one and then only so long as it takes his resourceful mind to design a way out of doubt. And
yet he sees the impressive rôle that doubt has
played in modern philosophy, and must play in
every life that does not stagnate. For this reason
he treats scepticism as itself one of the six major
methods of knowing. The five positive methods
he describes as: authoritarianism, mysticism, ra-
tionalism, empiricism, and pragmatism. Scepticism is negative, and is a method only, as he
says, ' in the sense that anarchism is a theory of
government, or atheism a kind of theology.' He
has tried to turn to positive account the negative
cast of this approach to reality by answering, as
well as exposing, all the major justifications offered for doubt as such. These efforts at justification he outlines in four arguments: the historical, the dialectical, the physiological, and the
psychological.

If the reader can endow himself with the good
fortune of perusing these weighty pages of Montague, he will see that we have been, for a practical reason, hardly more than playing with the
problem of doubt and assuming its solution. For
Montague gives in detail the various types of
doubt and in equal detail the variety of answers
that have been historically made. Moreover, he
evaluates the answers as well as the questions.
Since we are interested in his treatment of scepti-

cism primarily only as it reveals his own doubts, let us have done as quickly as possible with his historical conclusions and pass then to his treatment of his own personal doubts.

His major conclusion is that 'the historical, the dialectical, the physiological, and the psychological arguments do indeed show that the human mind is unable to attain absolute certainty in any field.' But 'absolute certainty' is a very large order, indeed; and between it and the 'blank indifference' of extreme scepticism, of the type we identified with Pyrrho, there is room for men who are not extremists both to stand and to live. Wise men will, then, forswear the luxury of certainty for the necessity of probability. Necessitated by the unavailability of the perfect, probability is not too bad as a guide to life. It is the task of a man to make probability rise toward certainty rather than sink toward ignorance. How real, however, is the difficulty involved in consummating even this more modest task, may be seen by remembering what it was about which Hume shocked the world of thought and science. It was the uniformity of nature which he imperilled by his attack upon causation as a necessary, dependable relation. It is upon this very uncertainty, indeed, that Montague is at last driven to rest his claim for probability. 'In short,' as he admits, 'our whole argument in refutation of scepticism stands or falls with our claim that a causal order in nature with its guarantee of a continuance of uniformity in the future, is at least possible as an hypothesis.'

To get thus out of a survey of all history only a mere possibility of knowledge seems modest indeed. And yet it is something to be able to take down from the doorway of hope 'the sceptic's despairing *ignorabimus*' and to write up in its stead the more cautious legend '*ignoramus*.' 'A failure to solve a problem,' Montague rings out, 'is not a proof of its insolubility.' The sceptic may, of course, be right: 'it remains conceivable that the sceptic's assertion that *nothing can be known* is really true even though all arguments in its favor are false.' But the sceptic may also be wrong. Possibility is something; it is what an honest mind admits when it cannot find anything more. But a brave man needs something more; he needs a probability to make energization for action worth while. Is there enough chance to justify an effort? In Montague's concise phrase, 'Granted that this is a *possibility,* what is its *probability?* '

III. Probability as Guide to Life

Now the first thing to be said about Montague at this crossroads, is that he is intellectually honest. He is in this respect hardly less than a modern Hume. I mean that he will not give himself or his hope, as such, the benefit of the doubt, will not dogmatize probability from proved possibility. It is easy to do just this, if you have less than a completely scrupulous mind. And that kind of mind is, alas, extraordinarily uncommon. About all the logic that most men need to prove what they want to believe is something like this: What I want to be true is not impossible, therefore it is possible, therefore it is probable, therefore it is likely — what more do I want? Let's go! Many men engage in such self-fooling without knowing better; but any trained mind that so engages in self-fooling is not at bottom scrupulous. Montague, I believe, is scrupulous. The *probability* of what is *possible* must itself be determined from facts, not hopes.

The second thing to be said about Montague at the delicate pass to which his discussion of scepticism has brought him, is that he is realistic and empirical in temper. If knowledge is a matter of probability, he wants to know what the probability is in any given case. ' Just how great is the probable truth of any given system,' — he concludes his historical discussion of scepticism — ' depends upon the number of its elements and the extent of their convergence of mutual corroboration.' That is, probability breaks up into probabilities, and these can be determined only by empirical acquaintance with what is in question. This does not mean that Montague has ceased to be a philosopher and has become a scientist. No, it does not mean this any more than — to anticipate the next chapter — Justice Holmes' feeling that in the law ' the black-letter man may be the man of the present, but the man of the future is the man of statistics ' — any more, I say, than this means that the Justice has deserted law for the science of statistics. But it does mean that, for both these and many others, ' the growth of education,' as Holmes put it, ' is an increase in the knowledge of measure.' Montague still devotes himself to such weighty philosophic questions as those of the ancient verities, God, Freedom, and Immortality, just as Holmes devotes himself still to the weighty matters of the law. But to even these questions Montague brings, as Holmes to those, the probability seeking mind. Montague has developed, as have few others in the field of philosophy, the habit of estimating the chances, rather than of proclaiming the certainties, where no certainty exists. To illustrate this habit of mind in several fields, we will do what is here possible to show how Montague uses intelligence to resolve doubts inflicted upon his mind by nature. And first, the dear old hope of immortality, dead as an issue for many modern minds, but not dead and very dear to Montague. As introduction to his seriousness on this point, we may say of him with reference to current negations of immortality what he says himself with reference to negations of

God: ' A man may well believe that this dreadful thing is true. But only the fool will say in his heart that he is glad that it is true.'

IV. ON ESTIMATING THE PROBABILITIES OF IMMORTALITY

We do not begin this discussion by pressing the antecedent question of whether there is a soul; for Montague's doubt from childhood as to the soul has never been so much *whether* as *where, how, how long*. And as for the smart mood avowing a distaste for an after life, well, that's no possible mood for Montague. ' Life's grateful rhythms,' as he observes against those who yield up faith from sheer fatigue, ' and cumulative hierarchies of successively more embracing purposes, with their alternations of novelty and familiar repetitions, are of life's very essence and need no terminus to make them sweet.' No, this lover of life feels sure that ' to praise oblivion as the only alternative to intolerable ennui is the mistake of a tired fancy.' I do not mean to suggest that Montague merely assumes the existence of the soul or that he argues that it must be because he or we would have it so. Far from either. For a fact, as I write these lines there comes to me his latest book, the Ingersoll Lecture, delivered at Harvard University, 1932, characteristically entitled *The Chances of Surviving Death*. In this

lecture Montague canvasses anew, and more
thoroughly than before, the whole question of
what the soul can be, to be so meaningful.

In highly critical mood regarding this deep
hope, he here takes Descartes to task for having
too cavalierly made his logic jump with his hopes.
From *cogito ergo sum* Montague does not see, any
more than we saw upon looking at the argument in
Chapter III, how logically one can get a substance
from an activity, unless the substance be smuggled
in from the beginning as a stowaway by hope. ' I
think, therefore I am ' — ' Yes,' says Montague,
' but am how, and am what? ' Taking sides with
Hume, he continues: ' All I *know* is that I exist
as conscious at this moment, but whether I exist
as a substantive, or as an adjective of something
else, is not to be discovered by any direct experience.' He makes clear in the discussion that he
thinks Descartes was pursuing the real issue, but
that he settled it too easily. Let us look more
carefully at Montague's own way of approaching
the question.

Is soul merely a quality of the body, he asks, as
music is of its instrument, vibrating, like sweet
music, only so long as the strings are struck? Then
too would the soul, like the ceasing of exquisite
music, fade into dear nothingness when the body
dies and friends forget. For numerous concrete
reasons he concludes against the likelihood that
the soul is a mere quality of the body or of any-

thing else. The alternative that remains, then, is that it is a quantity, a thing in its own right, with its persistence beyond the body's death still an open question. He is concerned to show, against what he regards as an artificial current mood, that ' there is nothing antiquated or unworthy about the question of man's personal continuance.' ' The chance of its being real,' he acknowledges, ' may be desperately slight, but in momentous importance the possibility of immortality is second only to the possibility of a cosmic personality in whom values . . . might possess an eternal ground.' The probability of God's existence we shall turn to presently, but for the moment let us pursue to the end the probable survival of the soul as substance.

Montague believes that the mind is a real entity, ' substantive ' he calls it, rather than a mere quality such as we have illustrated. But he does not believe even this like a devotee, because while he can work the hypothesis of survival up from a bare and sterile possibility to something like a *respectable* probability, he cannot make it appear an *overwhelming* probability. And things must be held to be what after our best consideration they seem to be. As a matter of fact Montague harbors in maturity a notion about the soul not without affinity with his childish fancy. He thinks it likely that the soul is a sort of immaterial material man inside each of us. He calls it ' an organism within an organism.' But dogmatically to declare that this ' insider ' indisputably survives death is beyond the range of his intellectual caution.

The queston is seen in his discussion to be very complex, to involve all that we know of physics and chemistry, and more than we know of biology and psychology. Moreover, it involves differentially such levels of being as are repre- sented by (1) an event, (2) a vegetable, (3) an animal, (4) mere man, and (5) superior man. Who but thoughtless man would seek to insure himself for eternity oblivious of the fate of all lower forms, especially of the dog whose devotion surmounts ' the sad barrier of species and of rank.' Not without distinguished company does Mon- tague suspect that ' there would be more point in continuance through eternity of the poor brute being who, despite the limitations of his mental span of comprehension, could go through pain and death for loyalty than there would be in the eter- nal continuance of the cleverest human rogue who ever lived.' Moreover, he does not neglect to indi- cate various possible degrees of survival, from mere continuance as a *has been,* through continu- ance as a quick and growing thing, to a ' mystic union with that greater Life ' who would minister to our finitude as to ' a sort of wound that cries for healing.' ' If that vaguely longed-for supple- ment to our being could come,' he concludes, ' and come without the annihilation of such being as we already have, then would eternity hold out to us the prospect of something unimaginably more than mere survival.' So much to indicate the temper and approach, rather than the rich content, of Montague's judicious argument. The probability, and even the full desirability, of the possibility of immortality is seen in the last quotation to have connection with another possibility, whose probability in turn we must now consider.

V. ON ESTIMATING THE PROBABILITIES OF GOD

Next to his concern with the soul, which to him is primarily a scientific and secular question, Montague acknowledges religion as his lifelong preoccupation. Religion he conceives, in characteristic fashion, as ' the possibility that what is highest in spirit is also deepest in nature.' But how come such faith? Given a soul, what are its reliances? ' The feelings of loneliness, insufficiency, and terror are the real drives that generate religion.' With this type of feeling as motivation, it is clear that Montague would no more be satisfied in religion by some vague humanism or secular idealism than he was satisfied by those willing to forego a soul or to dismiss the subsequent question of its immortality. To use his own pungent phrase caught in another connection, he could not ' swallow any such mess.' Nor is he to be intimidated into silence by mere changes of style in ideologies. Weather comes and goes, but the real climate of spiritual opinion is fairly uniform in a given culture. In ours most men will have God or they will know why not. From Plato to our day western aspiration has held to ' the ancient and pathetic hope that the world is somehow kind to us, and that the things for which we care most are not ultimately at the mercy of blind and indifferent forces.' This hope it is in Montague's opinion that ' impels the search for God.'

Now starting from this lowly level of fears and hopes, there are two problems that attract attention in considering the probabilities in favor of God. There is first what has long been called ' the problem of evil.' It has worried men no little as to how to harmonize their distant hopes of triumphant good with their immediate experience of evil riding here, like the rowdy cowboy, ' high, wide, and handsome.' ' Right forever on the scaffold, wrong forever on the throne. . . .' Montague is also sensitive to the implications of this all but universal quandary. His treatment of this problem of evil, however, we reserve to the next section. He is equally sensitive to certain opposed observations. In short, he poses as not only worthy of, but even exacting, consideration — what he calls ' the problem of good.' From concern with this aspect of the matter he finds his way to a faith in deity. This faith, too, never doubt, is based upon an estimate of probabilities rather than upon any certainties; but whoever has only probabilities on which to live learns to rate differential probabilities very highly. And this Montague does for God, in the following manner.

The problem of good arises from the presence of too much good in the world to be explained without the existence of God. More humbly put, to begin with, if the word is merely a mechanism, how come purpose? How come the dynamic upsurging called evolution, with its various levels? How come man at all?

> Has some Vast Imbecility,
>   Mighty to build and blend,
>   But impotent to tend,
> Framed us in jest, and left us now to hazardry?

How can such things be? The acceptance of miracles arising out of a mechanistic nature requires a brand of piety that is simply not natural. Anybody who could believe that out of a blind beginning by mechanical principles there could arise by chance such things as we see about us and in us, is prepared, thinks Montague, to believe in God — or to go to the insane asylum. ' Any such chance,' says he, ' would be so near zero as to be negligible.' Not that he proposes to settle the existence of God in any such cavalier fashion. But materialists and determinists ought to be shocked into seeing that they are as much on the defensive when it comes to explaining the good in the world, as idealists and spiritualists are when it comes to explaining the evil in the world. To put it summarily in Montague's latest words, 'The Problem of Good is insoluble in terms of traditional Atheism.'

This does not mean that there must be a God; for on what compulsion *must* any problem be solved, be it of good or of evil? But it does mean that if we want to make our world as rational as it might be, we must at least consider with an open mind the probabilities involved in and lying between these two dilemmas of too much good for chance and too much bad for God. Coming at the matter still from the presence of the anomalous good, what are the probabilities that there is a God who caused and causes what we call good? This question Montague considers carefully and answers in his Terry Lectures at Yale, 1930, now published as *Belief Unbound: A Promethean Religion for the Modern World.*

He acknowledges that from primordial elements of matter in motion things might arise, even complexities might occur. And who knows indeed that some very good structures might not here and there crop up? 'But that any considerable number of these higher aggregates would come about by mere chance would itself be a chance almost infinitely small.' Moreover, those that did arise by chance would by the same chance be constantly dissolved into their elements. Now that there is much dissolution in this very world is obvious. Organisms come and go, and even the towering pride of man yields, like all humbler forms, to death. True, without a doubt. But equally true is the fact that this pride of man provides for death with insurance, celebrates it with epitaphs and mausoleums, and even up to a point thwarts death by leaving progeny to carry on. What is more, below man even nature herself proliferates forms from forms and by preserved variations improves her breed as she moves along. The fact that this evolutionary process eventuates in man knowing good and evil, adds height to nature; but there is depth of plan and breadth of execution in the enormous complexities, self-sourced, self-maintaining, and self-perpetuating, that characterize nature even at her dumber levels. 'What is the chance,' Montague asks the atheist, 'that all this ascent is in a universe of descent, the result of chance?'

'Let the atheist lay the wager and name the odds that he will demand of us.' But let him first realize that it is this world with all its wonders and goods that is to be explained by chance. The chance would be small indeed that enough separate letters pitched into the air would arrange themselves by chance so as to spell out 'See the cat.' How much smaller the chance that they would spell out the whole play of, say, *Hamlet!*

But there is Shakespeare's mind of many plays and his personality that has stumped the world! Meditate further, my friendly reader, upon this line of thought, and then you will enter the spirit of Montague's guess that the atheist ' certainly will not bet with us on even terms.' Montague concludes: ' I am afraid that the odds that he will feel bound to ask of us will be so heavy that they will make him sheepish, because it is, after all, the truth of his own theory on which he is betting.'

Now it is clear enough what the alternative is to this — a god. I spell it thus, because it might not take a full-sized God to explain this kind of world. It is in spots a curiously bungled job, this world. But it is quite a job for mere unaided chance to have done. How big a god, and how good a god, is a matter to be decided on the merits of the case the world presents. Men differ upon those merits, of course, and so have always differed upon the job specifications for their divinity. But what they may differ less upon than heretofore is the need of some divinity to shape such cosmic ends, if only they are willing to estimate the probabilities of God as indicated by ' the problem of good.' ' If we are right,' he concludes in fatherly if paradoxical mood, ' we escape the universe of perpetual miracle, on which the atheist sets his heart.' But now for ' the problem of evil.'

VI. On Estimating the Probabilities of No God

To an optimistic reader it might seem that our religious troubles are now over, so far as we elect to follow Montague. Starting from the presence of the good that is in the universe, has he not found that a divinity is the most probable explanation of it? Yes, but that does not end our troubles; for an honest mind like Montague's cannot, after all, blink ' the problem of evil.' Truth to tell, there is along with the good too much unmitigated evil in plain sight to allow us to rest with the hypothetical god that we have achieved. No contemporary can point, or has pointed, with more arresting finger than Montague to the black patches on reality. It is as invigorating as it is rare to see a predominantly religious man blink no blotches upon what we shall presently see is the object of even Montague's devotion. Schopenhauer himself has drawn no more livid picture than this: ' On life itself has been put the curse, worthy of a primordial demon's genius, of having to feed upon itself, and carry on by murder and betrayal of its very own.' And then in defense of men like Schopenhauer, whom the race not infrequently disdains as nursing a grouch, Montague continues: ' Pessimists as yet have hardly scratched the surface of life's woe. I venture to believe that, should one ever come with the ability to give us in his writing a vivid first-hand sense of even a tithe of those agonies actually existing at a single moment, his words would burn our eyes blind, and melt the foulest hearts with pity.'

In the light of all this, the more certain we are of a god, and the more he grows in our probability to the stature of the God of religion, the more uneasy we become. For we are soon made to face something worse than all the evils we know on earth, draw those as black as we may; we are made to face the fact of evil in God's own character. For a God who is powerful enough to prevent evil and will not do it, is bad. And, on the other side, a God who would prevent evil and cannot, is not the God we fain would have as the companion of our hearts and the protection of our hopes.

We shall return to the second alternative presently. For the moment let us follow Montague in dealing with the first alternative. Montague disdains all the easy ways by which minds none too scrupulous or none too intelligent have handled the problem of evil. These ways are many. Unintelligent apologists will declare that we cannot judge God, while all the while judging in his favor. Montague cannot fool himself by denying that he is doing what he *is* doing, and he cannot stultify himself by judging good what, by all the tests he knows, is actually evil. And, for a fact, can anything be more evil than to be all-powerful and not use the power to cure and prevent evil? Yes, one thing could be more evil, and that is to use the power actually to cause evil. And God as creator invites this odium, as God the preserver invites the other. Intelligent apologists will assert that what seems evil to finite minds is not actually so when seen from the point of view of the universe or of the whole. As Alexander Pope long ago expressed it —

> All discord, harmony not understood,
> All partial evil, universal good.

This type of apology clearly obscures the plain fact, however, that for finite minds there is available no infinite point of view. In that event, Montague says with telling effect, ' the experience of what is alleged to be unreal evil becomes itself the real evil.' There seems to him no escape from the conclusion that ' if God's purposes are other than what we call good, then his nature is other than what we mean by good, while to go further and assume, as some absolute idealists have assumed, that our sin and agony actually contribute to God's enjoyment, would be to make him not merely lacking in good, but a demon of evil.' God must long ago have learned what it is to suffer at the hands of his friends — or are such apologists friends of God? — and have resigned himself to remain unknown rather than suffer the high pains of full exposure. Or is it as Thomas Hardy insinuates in his conversation with deity —

Said I: " We call that cruelty —
    We, your poor mortal kind."
He mused: " The thought is new to me.
Forsooth, though I men's master be,
Theirs is the teaching mind! "

Now Montague is convinced that these apologists, bad as they are, are as good as any, if God
is, as they severally assume him to be, genuinely
omnipotent. It is the assumption that is bad; and
being so, it corrupts the rationalizations. The
rationalization that we cannot judge God is self-
refuting, since in the very act of fabricating that
judgment we are judging him to be good. The
other apologies reduce, in Montague's opinion, to
this: ' If evil is really nothing, it is nothing to
avoid; while if it is some disguised or indirect form
of good, it is a duty to abet it, not oppose it.'
Indeed does it not also follow that ' we should
not only be " *willing* to be damned for the glory of
God," we should strive for it ' ? What, then, is
to be our judgment upon a line of argument that
at the best is either silly or vicious? The conclusion is easy: such argument must be in a bad
cause. That, indeed, is Montague's conviction.
God's power must once and for all be given up; it
will be given up gladly by a man of honor. Like
Prometheus of old, such men will joy to proclaim
abroad that ' the ideal outranks the power of
Heaven itself.' The belief in a God of power has
not only rendered God himself morally equivocal,

it has had very bad effects, oblique when not direct, upon the morals of worshippers. The social effects of tying up the whole moral life of man with an indefensible presupposition are nowhere more tellingly indicated than in Montague: ' Those who sow the wind of theological authority are destined to reap the whirlwind of ethical confusion in the generations that follow.' Upon these grounds, and others not here paraded, Montague draws this simple but momentous conclusion: ' there can exist no omnipotent God.' Such then is the pass to which this approach — through the problem of evil — has brought us.

Let us now take stock of our gains and losses. The probabilities arising from the problem of good have pointed us to *a* god; the moralities arising from the problem of evil have pointed us away from *the* God. What remains? There remains the deification pointed to by the other end of our dilemma: a god who would have done better than this world is but who could not. In short, the religious craving must content itself with a finite deity. We would give up God altogether rather than stultify our consciences; for ' atheism leads not to badness but only to an incurable sadness and loneliness.' We cannot keep our consciences unsullied and believe in an omnipotent God; for, as Montague pleaded in his concluding address to the Sixth International Congress of Philosophers, at Harvard, in 1926, we must ' prevent man from committing the sin against his own spirit, the unforgivable sin of subordinating the ideal to the real and accepting whatever is as therefore right.'

There is, however, somewhat more against atheism than the sadness and loneliness just alluded to; there is the integrity endangered by ignoring the probabilities. When probabilities are all we have, we cannot desert them with impunity; and especially can we not when, like these, they go some way toward reconciling what Montague calls ' the need of our heart with the cold and meagre knowledge of the facts of existence.' Let no one mistake the fact that this outcome is not what Montague would have wished. Such a deity, precious as he may be in being our very own, still leaves us at the mercy of fate in more ways than we like to contemplate. There is this final consolation: one can believe in such a God without sacrificing his moral integrity; he cannot refuse to believe in such a God, if he sees the probabilities as does Montague, without endangering his intellectual integrity.

VII. Tell Us More of this Finite Deity!

That God is weak we must now acknowledge; but that he is honest we can at last proclaim. What more? There are two things more, if in a brief compass I can but exhibit them as subjects of a unified discussion. The first of them is that the being of God is dependent upon the world's being itself an animal in some sense or other. The second is an hypothesis as to what kind of animal the world itself is. The first Montague himself has put explicitly: ' The only chance for the existence of anything worthy the appellation of Deity must turn on the possibility that the cosmos has a life and mind of its own. . . . In the old and unattractive words we may ask: Is there any likelihood that the world is an animal? ' Now this question Montague answers, again by means of probabilities, in affirmative terms. His analysis is thrilling and his reasons multiple, the latter reaching all the way from the new physics, which he understands as few philosophers understand it, to the oldest of common sense, whose humble cogency he also mightily commands. I hesitate to touch upon the matter here, since I can only touch upon it.

But perhaps the line of his thought may be ever so slightly suggested by noting his remark that the human brain, as the special habitat of thought, is one bit of matter that has a mind. Maybe other matter is dead, but the cerebral matter is living and somehow thinking. And yet the matter in the brain differs in no formidable way from other matter as matter. If, then, the brain can be so moved upon or endowed, why not other segments of matter, why not indeed the whole material universe? ' If sentience is based on matter ' — and Montague joins others in supposing that it is — ' it cannot be based merely upon some special distribution of its particles, it must rather be intrinsic to material being as such.' Now that line of reasoning need be only followed through to find the universe, if we may use now his ' unattractive words,' to find the universe itself an organism, a finite personality, indeed the very God to which the problem of good pointed the finger of probability. This is not pantheism — to such as demand a label — it is rather panpsychism.

It will be seen at once that this soul of the world is but the enlargement to cosmic scale of Montague's conception of the human soul as being a material immaterial counterpart of the body, depending upon the body, directing the body, but probably at last surviving the body. It will be seen, moreover, that this is but the maturation of the notion of the soul which Montague voiced, inopportunely if not prematurely, at his mother's knee. The world's soul is God. We were guided to him by the presence of good in the world. Since now, however, he *is* the world, on its inner side, he is brought almost uncomfortably close once more to evil. Why does he clothe himself with such a body? What is the nature of this cosmic deity, and what his intentions with reference to the blemishes upon his own body?

It is somewhat hazardous to try to answer the question on the basis of the evidence Montague has as yet given us. Further, and shortly forth-coming, evidence may modify or even refute what I am about to say. But pending the publication of his *The Great Visions of Philosophy,* I must indicate on the basis of the first chapter of that book, a chapter already published in *The International Journal of Ethics* (October, 1933), a most intriguing suggestion. It is that instead of regarding the universe as somehow Reason, as so many idealists have done, or as somehow Will, as Schopenhauer and some others have done, we regard it as Imagination. The advantages of this conception are not far to seek. Devotees of Reason as the cosmic stuff have faced without reasonable reply the irrational aspects of the world. Exponents of Will have lacked the will to do justice to what is actually reasonable in the world. Disciples of Imagination will find it easier to face both the aspects of reality than devotees of either the rational or the irrational aspect have been able to face the other.

For note how human imagination has its moments of creative joy, its moments of audacious heights, its moments of transcending beauties stretching out and up. But it has also its turn with phobias, and manias, and nightmares — all these

> Lonelier and dreadfuller than sunlight is,
>   And dumb and mad and eyeless like the sky.

What is so like both these sides of our inner life as is this queer world that we know? As regards its darker side, Montague is right in seeing what ' we happy and successful members of the conquering human race . . . forget ' — namely, ' that this mountain on which we live is a mountain of skulls, and that the failures, deaths, and miseries of our humbler brethren make up the purchase price of our estate.' But who, knowing this world of ours, will say that Montague is less right in seeing also ' some loveliness . . . everywhere. Great joys are had, and great ideals are successfully fulfilled. All life is shot with meanings, and probably non-life too, could we but see them . . . .' That is our Janus-faced world. But it is also true, as we have noted, that it is ' a vast, disorderly progeny that imagination bears, grotesques and monsters, horrible, trivial, and beautiful mingled indifferently. . . .'

Who, then, is prepared, seeing all this, to say that there is not plausibility in Montague's final fancy that ' the whole realm of nature, taken both individually and collectively, organically and inorganically, appears . . . unmistakably like the fruit of a World-Imagination ' ? At any rate, one can now understand a man whose fancy ' this dim vision haunts.' This is the man who saw — what he saw, on the bridge over the little brook, in California, more than twenty-five years ago. To him, ' existence is not a tale told by an idiot nor by a theologian; it is a tale told in many languages and not overly censored in any, such a tale as we might hear if all the eternal possibles of Being gave tongue at once in space and time, and raced together in pursuit of actuality.' Such a man, our friend and guide, we now understand, as we could not have before, when he assures us that ' the ways of imagination and vision are . . . man's nearest approach to the ways of primordial Being.'

VIII. A MODEST MORAL FROM MONTAGUE

I think you may, my patient reader, understand why I am somewhat abashed now that the time has come to draw my moral from this man Montague. His lines have been unique and satisfying. Morals, especially when drawn, are likely to be thin and meagre. But this moral must not be either thin or meagre, being as it is from Montague. In fact, perhaps I do not need to draw it at all. I have quoted as many of his fine lines as I possibly could. What he has to teach us is in those lines. I do not now refer to what he said, though that too. I refer to the way he said it, and the pervasive spirit of the saying. There is in this man something that makes him the William James of our generation. There is a humility that finds itself not abased in seeing lowly facts and in prizing forgotten nobodies. There is an audacity which will not be estopped at having or at voicing grand ideas in a manner quite as grand. There is a sincerity in holding to be good what he feels good and in daring to count so far true what is more probable than not. All this is there, none of it disconnected from doubts entertained and overgrown, all of it a function of his truth-seeking soul, doomed to accept probabilities as guide to life.

The further reason why I do not have to draw the moral is that Montague not only exemplifies it in whatever we quote from him but that he has also stated it. Two virtues he holds primary: courage and enthusiasm. Courage, one of the oldest prized and always deserving virtues, has been strangely lacking in ethics, the theory of the virtues. Life is essentially an adventure. And yet morality as the rationalization of the good life has too often concerned itself with duties which negated every adventurous element. Even where a duty-ethics has risen above parochial inhibitions, as in Kant, it has sought its genius in ' the law that there shall be law.' Now, according to Montague, morality is no such thing; its genius lies precisely in the opposite direction: ' it is *the law that there shall never be law,* but always a departure from law, a maximum of variation, innovation, and adventure.'

It is a slave morality that says Nay, everlastingly Nay, to life. Buddha voiced it, and Jesus was not free of defeatism. They both had ' courage of the heart ' — capacity to endure. That must we also have, but more — ' the new courage of the mind, the resoluteness to use intelligence. . . . ' We must overcome temperance, never a virtue — timorous cautions to the contrary — save in dealing with ' our sins and sorrows.' ' The notion that Temperance possesses intrinsic value,' declares Montague, ' is as false as it is ancient and as mischievous as it is respectable.' Who wants to be, or ought to be, temperate in his joys?

The exact opposite is the lead proposed by Montague in the name of courage. And here this basic virtue passes easily into what Montague calls its genius, but what is also clearly its fulfilment. For the greatest virtue is enthusiasm — ' all that makes for the hard work of actualizing potentialities.' On the analogy of an economic law of diminishing returns Montague enunciates for life and morals what he calls ' the Law of Increasing Returns.' This is his way of dramatizing the truth that good and evil gain by concentration and lose by dispersion. Evils should, therefore, be scattered as much as possible, as, for instance, we do through insurance. But the goods should be concentrated as much as possible, even, he suggests, to perhaps the point of well managed lotteries. At any rate, he feels certain that ' a single great beauty is worth more than many pretties; a major poet is worth more than his own weight of minor poets; a supreme ecstasy cannot be equaled by a number of little joys.'

Now what we need even beyond courage in order to act upon this conviction, is enthusiasm. This virtue alone can redeem courage from austerity and lift action above the stingy level of duty. ' Abandon ' is what we need on the positive side of life. ' To achieve happiness,' cries Montague, ' enthusiasm in the sense of abandon or concentrated intensity should replace temperance as the rule of virtue and true wisdom.' Here is at last a philosopher, who in no reckless mood but merely in the interest of making life what under God it ought to be and could be, urges us to go the limit. Who since William James has sounded a tocsin note save on behalf of caution? Montague will sound no note save in behalf of a fuller life. ' The rewards of " plunging," " going the limit," " draining the cup to the last drop," etc., are out of all proportion greater than those of safe half-hearted dabbling on the principle of nothing too much.' This, then, is the only attitude, that of unleashed enthusiasm, which is likely, in his opinion, ' to burn away the futilities, frivolities, and wastes that plague us today.'

Both these great virtues this affirmative minded sceptic has illustrated as well as preached; courage in declaring not only for life, when it is but timorously popular, but also for God, when he is not at all popular, and for immortality, when it is no longer seriously discussed among us. True, none of these, save life, have risen through his sceptical espousal, above the level of a may-be that might yet be. But the enthusiasm with which Montague has turned his mind to turning phrases for even these unpopular causes has made one of his probabilities as good as two actualities represented by lukewarmness. Who, indeed, would not prefer a probability embraced with enthusiasm to a certainty of good weakly voiced? Religion bodies forth, or obscures, what many regard as humanity's greatest goods. ' Taking religion as we took it,' let Montague finally say, ' we see at once that it is neither certainly and obviously true nor certainly and obviously false, but possibly true, and, if true, tremendously exciting.' Is not that word ' probability ' a strong, even a blessed word, my reader, when enunciated with enthusiasm? Scepticism, I need not further assure you, is a great philosophy when held by a Man.

CHAPTER VI

DOUBTING ONE'S WAY TO DEMOCRACY

Being a super-moral from Justice Holmes

We are now well out of the depths of doubt. Not that in the classic figure to which we are about to turn doubt has played less than a crucial rôle. Rather, from him this final praise of doubt: ' To have doubted one's own first principles is the mark of a civilized man.' But doubting in him has at last come of age. In the early doubters, there was too much of the heroic, the histrionic. Doubt had not yet taken its own measure and become a hardy virtue for the day's work and endurance. Even in Montague, as eager as he is to do and to dare, the sceptical spirit is not yet immaculately incarnated as character. Doubt is weakened for its final fruition wherever it is not wholly and fully taken for granted. The solidest heroism is the seemly endurance of the intolerable as a matter of course. Doubt does not become a virtue of this dimension so long as it remains merely a private reliance. It is only where it flowers as a social principle, doubting men but still tolerating them and their ways with inflexible good humor, doubting the universe, though still accepting it with unclenched fist. Then it is that doubt becomes not so much a virtue as just a necessity. And in no other modern has this development so symmetrically occurred as in the personality and the philosophy of Justice Oliver Wendell Holmes, voluntarily retired now at ninety from judicial service with the acclaim of a nation as a garland for his years.

I. Maturity through War

If one could know how such things as the outlook of this loftily hardy man are formed, one would know next to all that one needs to know for an all but fully wise life. It is clear that the determining influence in the character of Holmes was not birth and breeding in Boston. It is not likely that it was the borrowed blood of paternal wit, or pride, or learning. Harvard, great as she was and is, has no technique more dependable than earnest hit-and-miss for such ends as this. Any one of these lacking — for to be sure he graced and prized them all — and Holmes might have been otherwise; but all of these present and conjoined would not alone have produced this unique result. Far more likely they would have produced a snob, high at the top but thin at the edges and meagre throughout. Such things have been known to be from ancestry, nerves, and nurture no poorer than those of Holmes. He himself was later to remark in another connection, as recorded in Bent's biography, that ' civilized men who are nothing else are a little apt to think that they cannot breathe the American atmosphere '; and he has been heard by friends to ' thank God,' in appreciation of a raw burlesque, that he was ' a man of low tastes.'

Already, however, before college or the 'teens were over, this true Boston blue-blade was with his friend William James ' high-hatting ' the universe, a rather large victim, even then lying in wait for both upstarts. Poor old universe, dubbed by these who often indulged in the sport called by them ' twisting its tail,' dubbed by them, I say, ' our dilapidated old friend the Kosmos! ' Innocent of any humble want unsatisfied, secured from psychic depreciation by a felt social position and the fine sight of the world at his feet, what was to keep the young Holmes from the common fate of becoming another of the puffy nobodies that famous men so often sire?

What indeed was to prevent just that, especially since it appears that from the very beginning he had no lack of conceit in his own powers? Emerson, friend of the father, had given the boy dangerous, even if valuable, advice. Wendell confided, according to Bent, that he was reading Plato. ' You should hold Plato at arm's length,' advised Emerson. ' Say to him: " You have been pleasing the world for two thousand years; see whether you can please me." ' Upon reading later at Wendell's request an essay upon Plato from the youth, Emerson mused out loud: ' Yes, you have done very well, but you haven't killed Plato. When you shoot at a king you must kill him.' The Justice is known to have said in subsequent years that he could write all he knew on half a sheet of note paper, but that he would want to reserve the other half so as to write on it, ' I'm not sure! ' Such youthful conceit with such sceptical potentialities would require chastening unless together they were to end their possessor in either intellectual frivolity or in complete and paralyzing doubt. What was to safeguard the genius of the sapling, to save it from the underbrush, and head it toward the skies and stars?

What indeed save danger, the breath of defeat, the scent of death? — only these as crucible could refine gold from the cultural tinsel and the personal conceit of the youthful Holmes. ' Some teacher of the kind,' Holmes has judged, ' we all need . . . in order that we may remember all that buffoons forget.' For William James, the teacher was a psychic ' fault ' that, opening as a fissure, disclosed stark unreason as nigh neighbor to his pride. Drawing slowly back from the sight of insanity, through the prolonged pain of hypochondria, James shed his trappings and in spite of learning became a Man. Nature had provided in Holmes no such defective temperament as painful means to save him from softness. Hardier than

James, solider, bolder, Holmes required medicine worse than any psychic unease to make nursling into man. War was his medicine.

Who will deny that but for the Civil War Holmes might well have gone through life impaired by that disease as fatal as it is paradoxical? — the disease of over-health, spiritual *polycythemia zera,* as the doctor would say. You, my reader, as a lover of peace, may deny it; but not so the boy's famous father, not so his intimate friends, not so Holmes himself. He himself lived to voice the conviction that such hardship ' is much fitter to make a man than for a youth to have at twenty all the luxuries of life poured into a trough for him.' And again he says: ' The stern experience of our youth helped to accomplish the destiny of fate.' At the dedication of the Northwestern Law School Building, in 1902, Holmes generalized these impressions from youth into a philosophy of the strenuous life: ' every joy that gives to life its inspiration consists in an excursion toward death.' His whole life was indeed to exemplify his further maxim, that ' no result is easy which is worth having.'

According to Holmes and his friends, easily wise with an after-wisdom, when this brave, cultured lad of twenty marched away from Boston and Harvard, from sweetheart and father, in 1861, he marched to his own making. Foresight indeed had it that the gallant Twentieth Massachusetts Regiment went to save the Union, even to free the slaves. Be that as it may. But hindsight has it that at least one soldier in that regiment — the young Oliver Wendell Holmes — went to save himself, went to free a great soul from succulence, went to meet fate, to accept a universe, to become at last a Man. I do not wish to exaggerate the influence of war upon Holmes, but it is certain that there is even more truth than humor in his own remark that ' since 1865 there hasn't been any biographical detail ' to his life.

It is a hard saying that men grow souls only through suffering. And it is a mean saying when used as an excuse for increasing the sum of inevitable woe. But it is a true one: a sort of truth of that stern nature which Holmes has declared to have ' but one judgment on wrong conduct . . . the judgment of death.' Notified of his promotion to a first lieutenancy, it is said, while he was reading old Thomas Hobbes' *Leviathan,* Holmes came back from the war with five bullet wounds to remind him at first hand and for good what Hobbes had written into that hard book, that might has a way about it which mere right somehow and forever lacks. War puts all men up against what is too much for any of them. The way in which they, especially if young, come to terms with this all-too-much is likely to determine how they will ever afterwards come to terms with the unending succession of the much-too-much that life constitutes and gives. Studying medicine abroad in his own youth, the elder Oliver Wendell Holmes reported some moral equivalent for what his son was to learn from war. ' I have,' wrote he, ' more fully learned at least three principles since I have been in Paris: not to take authority when I can have facts; not to guess when I can know; not to think a man must take physic because he is sick.'

The young Oliver Wendell Holmes, though no medical man like his father, learned to give rougher medicine than that meant by his father when the latter once said that mankind would be better off if all the vials were poured into the ocean, but woe to the fishes! Woe indeed in war to the poor fishes who must stand in the way of duty of the son who later upon occasion could not but recall ' that swift and cunning thinking on which once hung life or freedom — Shall I stand the best chance if I try the pistol or the sabre on that man who means to stop me? Will he get his carbine free before I reach him, or can I kill him first? ' But harder than to learn to give the medicine called for by the cancerous disease of war was it to take whatever medicine life inexorably prescribed.

That this young soldier learned ' to take it,' however, cannot be doubted. Wounded through the chest at Ball's Bluff, fatally it was supposed by both others and himself; shot through the neck

at Antietam, again within a hair's breadth of
death; shattered, like Achilles of old, in the
heel, at Chancellorsville — this young Bostonian
learned that at any rate war is no mere state of
mind. It involves and compels devotion to duty
as means, without the chance to raise ever anew,
as does the intellectual dilettante, the previous
question of ends. It is in time of stress a ' moving on in obedience to superior command, to certain and useless death.' It is, upon occasion and
that occasion determined by others than oneself,
to be ' thrown away ' for ' a bit of bunting,' if, as
Holmes says, you ' insist on prose.' But it is also
to learn not to insist on prose: to learn that the
' bit of bunting ' is a *flag*, whose red is ' our life-
blood,' whose stars are ' our world,' whose blue is
' our heaven.' War is indeed no mere state of
mind. It is seeing those die, again and again,
whose ' death seems to end a portion of our life
also.' It is to stifle ' the cynic force with which the
thoughts of common-sense will assail . . . in
time of stress.'

Learning to take it, as he did, this soldier, fortunately for us, learned also how to say it. What
confrontation of the crass forces of military realism
does to a sensitive man has never been better
expressed than by Justice Holmes in a subsequent
speech. ' If you have advanced in line,' he begins,
' and have seen ahead of you the spot which you
must pass where the rifle bullets are striking; if

you have ridden by night at a walk toward the line
of fire at the dead angle of Spottsylvania, where
for twenty-four hours the soldiers were fighting
on the two sides of an earthwork, and in the morning the dead and dying lay piled in a row six deep,
and as you rode had heard the bullets splashing in
the mud and earth about you; if you have been on
the picket-line at night in a black and unknown
wood, and have heard the spat of the bullets upon
the trees, and as you moved have felt your foot
slip upon a dead man's body; if you have had a
blind fierce gallop against the enemy, with your
blood up and a pace that left no time for fear —
if, in short, . . . you have known the vicissitudes
of terror and of triumph in war, you know that
there is such a thing as the faith I spoke of. You
know your own weakness and are modest; but
you know that man has in him [this is the major
element of the faith he spoke of] that unspeakable
somewhat which makes him capable of miracle,
able to lift himself by the might of his own soul,
unaided, able to face annihilation for a blind
belief.'

Yes, war it was that taught Holmes ' all too
hard,' as he expressed it in a poem, ' the inscrut-
able decree.' But it taught him more than merely
that might will have its way. ' Man's destiny is
battle,' he says of life and peace, ' and he has to
take the chance of war . . . sooner or later we
shall fall, but meantime it is for us to fix our

eyes upon the point to be stormed, and to get there if we can! ' Subsequent memories of even crass might on the field of action ' add a glory to the bare fact that the strongest legions prevailed.' Mind triumphing over fate adds ' that little touch of the superfluous which is necessary. Necessary as art is necessary, and knowledge which serves no mechanical end. Superfluous only as glory is superfluous, or a bit of red ribbon that a man would die to win.' Routine may be lifted to meaning by a song, and horror may become romantic when touched to symmetry by the habiliments of imagination. Concluding a reference to his generation, like himself, moulded in the crucible of war, Holmes says: ' We who have seen these men can never believe that the power of money or the enervation of pleasure has put an end to them. We know that life may be lifted into poetry and lit with spiritual charm. . . .'

Going out, then, at the beginning of the war, with a regiment that, in Holmes' phrase, ' never talked much about itself but that stood in the first half-dozen of all the regiments of the North for number killed and wounded,' our soldier-for-life came back with the maturity of acceptance written upon his brow and the grace of quietness to adorn his tongue forever afterwards. Upon the death, many years later, of one of his old colonels, Holmes mused to himself, ' the Twentieth has shrunk to a skeleton, a ghost, a memory, a forgotten name which we other old men alone keep in our hearts.' But this too he found himself able to accept, though it meant oblivion as the human goal: ' And then I thought: it is right. It is as the colonel would have had it.' The grace wherewith to consummate this final acceptance, the final human acceptance of oblivion, Holmes derives, characteristically, from the war: 'This also,' says he, ' is part of the soldier's faith: having known great things, to be content with silence.'

The same theme recurs in the poem read by Holmes at the first reunion of his Harvard class, after his part in the war was done —

> Let others celebrate our high endeavor
>> When peace once more her starry flag shall fling
> Wide o'er the land our arms made free forever;
>> We do in silence what the world shall sing.

To suffer what must be suffered and to do great things without noise or subsequent boast, this is a man's best covenant with fate and fame. Nor is it ' well for soldiers to think much about wounds.' The only fame, indeed, which fate can give with its wounds which counts is a fame of substance not of adjective. To watch the grandstands is completely to dissipate all worthy energies, the pure gold of all our being. (The Justice is said to have made it a lifelong rule not even to read the newspapers.) The encomia of men are too short-lived for the truly prideful. Ambition should be made of sterner stuff. ' No man has earned the right to intellectual ambition until he has learned to lay his course by a star which he has never seen, to dig by the divining rod for springs which he may never reach.' Ambition should, indeed, be made of sterner stuff, for longer vistas. ' Sooner or later the race of men will die; but we demand an eternal record.' And where, pray, is the substance so prized by men that they take from fellow men the poor substitute of adjectives? ' We have it,' he continues. ' What we have done is woven forever in the great vibrating web of the world. The eye that can read the import of its motion can decipher the story of all our deeds, of all our thoughts. To peruse the story of past events is to do homage to the elements that went to its making, and to con over books is to draw the sacred curtain behind which lie enshrouded the dreams dreamed by other men but badly damaged at the birth. So with us: our worthy fame is our well performed functions so inter-threaded with the functions of others as to lose us in the creation of the web of life and of history.'

This indifference on the part of the great Justice to the passing opinions of contemporaries is thus seen to represent not genuine disdain for other men. It means, the rather, that he gives other men themselves a status more substantial than to be sounding boards of his self-esteem, reserving, meantime, for himself a dignity above and beyond that of reputation. At the last, sees he, men can ' live only in the tissue of their work.' This work, moreover, when it is most likely to endure is not done in the company of others. ' A man of high ambitions,' says he, ' must leave even his fellow adventurers and go forth into a deeper solitude and greater trials. He must start for the pole. In plain words he must face the loneliness of original work. No one can cut out new paths in company. He does that alone.' But, as in Plato, the denizens of the den call also, and one must divide his time between the call of the wilds of wistfulness and originality and the pressing calls of fellow men.

This substantial acceptance of fellow men is, in fact, the second cardinal virtue that Holmes brought home from the war. Who indeed shall say that it is not more difficult a lesson, more profound a virtue, than his accepting the universe with quiet reverence? All men accept the universe — ' Egad, they'd better! ' True, not all accept it, as did Holmes, like a gentleman. Some take it lying down, resigned to whatever comes. Some take it with raised voice, defying gods and devils. Some take it dumbly, querying neither whence nor whither. Some take it wide-eyed, a-wonder at all that is, a-twitter at what may be. Some take it equivocally, today aflame, tomorrow hardly a flicker, day after tomorrow dumb despair. Holmes himself in this deeper regard is glad to confess some spiritual affinity with the Puritan — his friends say Stoic. ' Even if our mode of expressing our wonder, our awful fear, our abiding trust in face of life and death and the unfathomable world has changed,' writes he, ' yet at this day, even now, we New Englanders are still leavened with the old Puritan ferment . . . the cold Puritan passion is still here.' For Holmes more than for Millay, its authoress, are these lines —

> Feed the grape and bean
>   To the vintner and monger;
> I will lie down lean
>   With my thirst and my hunger.

It is this austerity in Holmes — Puritan or Stoic, as you will — that resents as silly the use of ' the energy that is furnished to us by the cosmos to defy it and shake our fist at the sky.'

But has Holmes with the same equanimity accepted the harder yoke — his fellow men? Perhaps not with the same; but certainly he has accepted them, and not without magnanimity. The notion is common that the Justice is a liberal, and it is not an unheard opinion that he is a humanitarian. The latter ought perhaps to be categorically denied, whatever we may in the event be led to think of the former. The suspicion is strong that some other term than love would the better describe his attitude toward humanity. But, thanks again to the wager of battle, it may be said for certain that he does not count men out, simply waive them aside, as such a son of Boston, graduated at Harvard, might have done. It was the war, indeed, as the context of the following remark makes clear that first taught him the relative irrelevance of rank: ' In the great democracy of self-devotion private and general stand side by side.'

Pursuing this matter of his social attitudes, ' the deepest cause we have to love our country,' says Holmes, ' is that instinct, that spark, that makes the American unable to meet his fellow man otherwise than simply as a man, eye to eye, hand to hand, and foot to foot, wrestling naked on the sand.' There are indeed those — such as contribute neither ' thought nor beauty to life ' — on whom he ' would let Malthus loose;' but they are the exceptions and his excoriation of them is not to be taken without the pinch of salt supplied by the manner of it. His acceptance of men includes even his enemies, and this virtue he attributes specifically, not to the Gospels, which he says bid men to make ' the vain attempt to love one's neighbor as one's self,' but rather again to the march and camp. ' The experience of battle soon taught its lesson even to those who came into the field more bitterly disposed.' Can one avoid seeing in that a self-reference to this son of Boston, graduated at Harvard? At any rate, Holmes continues: ' You could not stand up day after day in those indecisive contests where overwhelming victory was impossible because neither side would run as they ought when beaten, without getting at last something of the same brotherhood for the enemy that the north pole of a magnet has for the south — each working in an opposite sense to the other, but each unable to get along without the other.'

This lesson learned and added to his acceptance of the universe, not much perhaps remains to be learned of general wisdom for life. At least for our present exposition, these two need only to be generalized into a view, if not a theory, of truth, and then applied to the specialized action in which Holmes himself has participated as his social calling — to make complete this tale of Holmes as guide to life. He became convinced that opposition is necessary, that struggle is inevitable, and that all things inevitable are somehow right. But opposition must be otherwise resolved where it cannot be composed. Here enters the tragic sense of life. For not all opposition can be composed. Conflicting interests are as real in life as harmonious interests, and can certainly not be talked away, as idealists and even liberals too easily tend to assume. There are always among a free people those who will not knuckle under without a fight and who will not ' run as they ought when beaten.' Somebody has got to get himself killed now and then in order that the world may have

any peace; and any adequate stab at the truth
about life has to include that fact and make it
plain. From the battlefield, or somewhere near it,
therefore comes Holmes' notion of truth itself.
' I used to say when I was young,' he later avows,
' that truth was the majority vote of that nation
that could lick all others.' This is a view to which
the Justice still adheres with qualifications to be
developed presently.

II. Lessons of War Turned to the Uses of Peace

In passing from the elemental stresses that
matured Holmes, to a consideration of the larger
social world which he himself has done so much
to make, we can do no better than to pass on the
bridge which he himself has provided. Speaking
to friends upon his acceptance of the Associate
Judgeship of the Supreme Court of the United
States, he said: ' To have the chance to do one's
share in shaping the laws of the whole country,
spreads over one the hush that one used to feel
when one was awaiting the beginning of a battle.'
And his resolution to do the work as Justice which
we now know that he has done, echoed also the
language and resolution of the battlefield, where
his moral preparation had been completed. ' We
will not falter,' he said, facing his new judicial
duties. ' We will not fail. We will reach the earth-

works if we live, and if we fail we will leave our spirit in those who follow, and they will not turn back. All is ready. Bugler, blow the charge.' With that he left Massachusetts as a long favored son, to become the equally renowned son of a great nation and one of its strongest contenders for the fame that men call immortal.

It is the unique vocation and responsibility of that high court to which he went for a long hard service to choose the direction of our national life and in some degree to chart the nation's course. This has been denied by some judges, especially the responsibility of charting the national course. No such denial has come, however, from Holmes. He has courage for the full responsibility of his eminent station and honor to avow the truth as he sees it. This man who first met what James in a letter to him called ' the nudity of the Kosmos ' on the field of battle and there accepted this world as *his* world had thereafter nothing to shirk from, not even the truth. Conservative commentators and even other judges may confine the Court to logical deduction from the Constitution but not so Holmes. Wise to ' the fallacy of logical form,' he knows that they also create who merely sit and interpret. He warns that judges themselves must be responsibly on guard if they are to escape the perfection of fixity and safeguard the indigenous viability of the Constitution. Those who created the Constitution charted the initial course of the nation; the judges who re-create the Constitution, by deciding what can and what cannot be done under it, do but re-chart and thus continuously direct our ship of state. In the light of their frequent denial of what they clearly do, Holmes once remarked that 'Judges are likely to be naif, simple-minded men, and they need something of Mephistopheles.' Whatever may be said of Holmes himself as a Judge, it cannot be said that he is naif; whatever may be denied of him as human being, it cannot be denied that he has a touch of the Mephistophelean in his nature.

When therefore the debate has waxed warm as to whether judges help create the law or merely interpret the Constitution, Holmes has always been frank to admit the complicity of himself and colleagues in the process of fate. 'Behind the logical form,' he says, 'lies a judgment as to the relative worth and importance of competing legislative grounds, often an inarticulate and unconscious judgment, it is true, and yet the very root and nerve of the whole proceeding.' Moreover, he has urged upon his judicial colleagues the acceptance of the responsibility for what he declares will be worse done if not done knowingly. 'I think that the judges themselves,' he continues, 'have failed adequately to recognize their duty of weighing considerations of social advantage. The duty is inevitable, and the result of the often proclaimed judicial aversion to deal with such considerations is simply to leave the very ground and foundation of judgments inarticulate, and often unconscious, as I have said.'

Seeing, then, the pivotal place held by Holmes and the responsible way he treats his station, let me suggest the vistas of this man's influence upon our national philosophy. I shall not try to make a completely systematic philosopher out of a man who is only philosophic in temperament, but I shall under the following three heads indicate an intellectual landscape that all wise men have surveyed with respect, many with great admiration: (1) Truth of nature and truths of man, (2) the tragic call of creative action, and (3) tolerance of action as the domestication of struggle.

III. TRUTH OF NATURE AND TRUTHS OF MAN

That this mild Mephistopheles of the modern temper has been a great doubter is not itself now to be doubted. He is the child of doubt in an age of science. ' Science,' he says, ' has taught the world scepticism and has made it legitimate to put everything to the test of proof.' And for himself he is convinced that ' a man should be able to criticize what he reveres and loves.' But that this sceptical spirit has recognized a limit in the accepted universe we have already seen. This limit includes also a final niche for man's existence as salvaged from doubt. ' Although I cannot prove

that I am awake,' Holmes puts the matter, in a
manner reminiscent of Descartes, ' I believe that
my neighbors exist in the same sense that I do, and
if I admit that it is easy to admit also that I am in
the universe, not it in me.' This geniality does but
point the way to a more austere respect for the
cosmos back of man, the source of man's truth as it
is of man's existence. ' The truth to me,' he once
remarked, ' is what I can't help but believe; but
I do not suppose that my can't helps are compul-
sory for the universe.' Accepting the universe as
is, he is absolved from longer shouldering responsibility for it. To him the universe as a whole,
which of course is unknowable, either is or contains the Truth as a whole. And it is the part of
wisdom to admit this and to respect if not also to
reverence the universe.

To acknowledge the universe, however, as
source of Truth does not mean to delegate to it
the administration of what we ourselves have built
in our little oasis, the world. For the Truth of
the universe is not our truth, nor can acceptance
of the universe, wise as that be, constitute an apology for our not taking our truths in hand, form-
ing them as we will, and realizing them as we can.
' There is every reason,' he often repeats in various
forms, ' for doing all that we can to make a future
such as we desire. The larger perspective of cosmic Truth but glorifies dull details and uplifts and
sustains weary years of toil.' The Judge in this

mood is fond of quoting George Herbert's beautiful lines —

> Who sweeps a room as for Thy laws,
> Makes that and the action fine.

But for this larger sweep, Holmes would appear to be a pure pragmatist, and no doubt he is a pragmatist, as far as pragmatism goes. Now, pragmatism may go all the way, as James sometimes seemed to do, to an inexorable universe which is there and constitutes a Truth which, while we can only approximate it, we must nevertheless respect as final. But when pragmatism stops short of that, holding rather the ' workability of ideas ' *to be* their truth, Holmes seems quietly to assume, as before, a cosmic truth which is the Truth of *that* truth and the limit of it. We may, then, call him a pragmatist or a pragmatist plus, depending upon what and whose pragmatism is in question. Specifically for him, the ' workability of ideas ' becomes the *test*, but not the *meaning*, of truth. Such is the import, taken in its setting, of the famous remark of the Justice that ' the best test of truth is the power of thought to get itself accepted in the competition of the market.'

This Truth beyond truths, however, let it be remembered, is not to be substituted compensatorily for our responsibility for our truths. Specifically Holmes disclaims such use of metaphysics: ' I do not see any rational ground for demanding

the superlative — for being dissatisfied unless we
are assured that our truth is cosmic truth, if there
is such a thing. . . . We still shall fight . . . for
the joy of it, and we may leave to the unknown the
supposed final valuation of that which in any event
has value to us.'

This same discrepancy — between final Truth
and truthly conveniences — Holmes remarks again
and again in the law. ' The truth is,' as he in one
place says, ' that the law is always approaching
and never reaching consistency. It is forever
adopting new principles from life at one end, and
it always retains old ones from history at the other,
which have not yet been absorbed or sloughed off.
It will become entirely consistent when it ceases to
grow.' In another place he exhibits the law (especially the law of Agency) as ' a conflict at every
point between logic and good sense ' — the one
striving for final consistency, the other for convenience. Still again he identifies the law roughly
with what at any time is conceived as the convenient. And, finally, he says: ' The prophecies of what
the courts will do in fact, and nothing more pre-
tentious, are what I mean by the law.' And though
the Court may not know it or may obscure it by
the logical language of certainty, its decision in a
really moot case, the Justice remarks, ' can do no
more than embody the preference of a given body
in a given time and place.'

To keep human truths (including law) from becoming stiffly perfect out of sympathy with that finality, Truth, which we may reverence but can never know, — this is the crux of the philosophical problem which has been the Justice's lifelong personal problem. Of this he is certain, ' the moving waters are full of life and health; only in the stagnant waters is stagnation and death.' But how to move with the river without being lost in the river, this is the crux. Holmes' own devotion, like a soldier under orders, to the Truth which soldiering taught him, is the source of that austerity which on the inside gives him direction and on the outside invests him with grandeur. His devotion, like an adventurer without orders, to the challenge of growth as the final call of life, is the source of that pliability which has endeared him to many who do not understand him. And, truth to tell, it is a great service to a nation to be taught in example as well as by such frequent precept that adventure to the disciplined is liberty; to the undisciplined, license. Holmes' life is a living moral to those disciplined enough to understand it. Holmes himself, however, is none too kind to those not fitted to understand him. He hesitates to extend to all the therapy of scepticism, that priceless cleansing power in his own life. ' When the ignorant are taught to doubt,' he observes, ' they do not know what they safely may believe.' For Holmes himself, however, we may now finally say that the path to fruitful discipline through doubt has become, on the one side, the tempered resolution of metaphysical yearning and, on the other side, the philosophy of government which his decisions enshrine. The key word to the double function is ' action,' and that key we now propose to turn both ways, in the hope of further treasures from the old warrior's chests.

IV. THE TRAGIC CALL OF CREATIVE ACTION

I speak advisedly of the ' tragic ' call to action. For, on the one side, Holmes says that ' life is action, the use of one's powers; ' but, on the other side, ' we cannot live our dreams. We are lucky enough if we can give a sample of our best.' In his many emphases upon action Holmes but illustrates the truth that it is not the workers of the world who raise peans of praise in favor of action. Leisure for them, and rest. Action for the ' intellectuals.' But action comes hard for the soft muscles that need it most, and especially such action as can shock men into tolerance for ways of life radically opposed to their own. War is no wishy-washy thing; it is a hell which men do not ordinarily elect *for themselves*. But it was a hell, which, in retrospect, Holmes saw as a rugged path to personal salvation: tragic but truth-leading. Another young intellectual — Rupert Brooke, this time — in 1914, marched away from another Cambridge, as Holmes had from his Cambridge, in 1861 — marched to the same newly discovered conviction:

Now, God be thanked Who has matched us with
    His hour,
And caught our youth, and wakened us from
    sleeping,

   .   .   .   .

Glad from a world grown old and cold and weary,

   .   .   .   .

And half-men, and their dirty songs and dreary . . .

From the rigor and wounds of war, the one of
these two youths who returned, brought back a
conviction not only of the inevitability but also of
the fertility of the struggle. ' After all,' declares
the soldier, ' the place for a man who is complete
in all his powers is in the fight.' This abiding emphasis we have already sufficiently noted. Competitive action discovers to us the enemy as a man;
it discovers us to ourselves as more than we previously had known; it tests our truths in the crucible
of time; and it either makes us, or makes for us,
leaders for heroic enterprises. Holmes confesses
that since some must have command (in our in-
dustrial life, the context has it), he knows ' no
way of finding the fit man so good as the fact of
winning it in the competition of the market.' (This
has not always worked out satisfactorily when the
' command ' was won in the ' stock ' *market*.) All
this we have seen as the philosophy of this, our
present guide to life. To maintain competitive action and to safeguard its perpetuity as the majority
principle, becomes the major end of law. This we

shall presently see. But just now what we are to see is that action, the more heroic the surer, may become man's, as it has Holmes', escape from scepticism and the incertitude which the modern mood provokes.

Holmes tells us anew that ' life is an end in itself and the only question as to whether it is worth living is whether you have enough of it.' Note how he applies this personal preference for action to the function of resolving doubt. ' War,' writes he in terrible earnestness, ' when you are at it, is horrible and dull. It is only when time has passed that you see its message was divine.' For either it or ' some teacher of the kind,' he goes on to declare, ' we all need. . . . We need it everywhere and at all times. For high and dangerous action teaches us *to believe as right beyond dispute things for which our doubting minds are slow to find words of proof.*' We've seen already another phrase to this same import, ' *blood up and a pace that left no time for fear.*' These several emphases seem so nearly the secret of the morale of this modern doubter that I have ventured to italicize them. Here indeed, experience will certify, is one way to certitude; it is the precipitous route of to do and to dare. The narrowed perspective which action imposes constitutes a kind of ' practical absolute,' which, if we can accept it as a pathway to the absoluteness of truth, is redeemed from its painful narrowness by the sacredness of its promise.

But is there any guarantee of this, its promise?
Let Mussolini say so. Let Stalin say so. Let
Hitler say so. Let the so-saying come in chorus
from all impetuous ones who prize relief from their
inner tensions enough to identify this paltry, but
precious, personal thing with absolute truth and
goodness. From only those let it come. Not from
Holmes. From him, rather, that ' certitude is not
the test of certainty,' that ' certainty generally is
illusion, and repose is not the destiny of man.'
Such abuse of the modern attitude and method of
doubt as represented by these Yea-sayers, has
brought modernism into disrepute in many quarters. The disrepute is not just; but it is sobering
— sobering beyond the intentions of those who
enunciate it as a call to retreat. For they who
thus abuse scepticism are but the re-incarnations
of those who have made of the best in every age
the worst, by committing against their own spirits
the unpardonable sins of stupidity or dishonesty
or of both. No system can stand when judged by
its worst.

But can our scientific-sceptical-industrial age,
which Holmes articulates, stand when judged by
its best? Well, it can certainly stand comparison
with the best of any other system. But not even
it can survive unsullied a comparison with utopia.
Justice Holmes himself, returning to the theme of
the foregoing italics, declares with hope, but a
hope corrected with honesty in the same breath,

that 'the proof comes later, and even may
never come.' The rub indeed's just there for
scepticism: *the proof may never come!* What
then?

Then, first, the catharsis of confession: ' it may
never come.' That confession Holmes, like a true
modern, has made; and that woundless pride in
self he has as a result. ' The real confession,' he declares however, ' is that the part cannot swallow
the whole — that our categories are not, or may
not be, adequate to formulate what we cannot
know.' Then, second, a declaration of personal
policy in the face of fate. This also Holmes proceeds to give. Note that it begins with ' therefore,' and know that it comes immediately after
the phrase ' it may never come.' ' Therefore,' so
runs the conclusion of the foregoing passage, ' I re-
joice at every dangerous sport which I see pursued.
The students at Heidelberg, with their sword-
slashed faces, inspire me with sincere respect.' If
this seems barbaric to you, my peaceful reader,
just remember that Holmes, like his friend James
in ' The Moral Equivalent of War,' sees war permanently necessitated *on moral grounds*, unless we
can make some replica of it widely available as at
once a discipline for the spirit and an outlet for the
surplus energy of men. Polo he also mentions in
this connection, and then comes the moral in his
own words: ' If once in a while in our rough riding
a neck is broken, I regard it, not as a waste, but as

a price well paid for the breeding of a race fit for leadership and command.'

But is this all — a life of strenuous action with a feeling of certitude in the wake of action, but with no guarantee that the feeling itself is not false? We ask Holmes, in poignant lines modified from Dunbar —

> Just flying, dreaming, dying so,
> The actors in the drama go —
> A flitting picture on a wall,
> Life, Death, the themes; but is
>   that all?

And Holmes answers back with humility befitting a sceptic that ' the universe has in it more than we understand, that the private soldiers have not been told the plan of campaign, or even that there is one, rather than some vaster unthinkable to which every predicate is an impertinence.' He answers that back, but adds in softer key: ' It is enough for us that the universe has produced us and has within it, as less than it, all that we believe and love.' It is a beautiful answer, and honest. But where does it leave us with reference to a criterion for action?

We insist upon that question, because the pragmatists have been accused of glorifying action for its own sake. And we have led ourselves to believe that Holmes is either just a plain pragmatist or a pragmatist plus. Does he glorify action for its own sake? If not, for the sake of what? For he

certainly glorifies action. If you have forgotten
that, let him assure you again that he ' knows of
no true measure of men except the total of human
energy which they embody. . . .' Moreover, the
words have hardly faded from your retina in which
he praises action as a cure, if not the cure, for general doubt. We remind ourselves, however, that
actually doubt is authentically cured only by getting to its proper object, desired but wanting. Now
the counsel of action seems to propose a substitute
object as distraction and compensation; it seems
to propose the *doing of something strenuous*, not
the gentle sitting down to think the matter through,
in order to see whether the doubted be real or
erroneous.

Perhaps in pressing the question — for we really
want to know — we ought to get into the picture a
middle-ground between these sharp alternatives.
It is a view sometimes credited to the pragmatists,
and not impossibly somewhere espoused by some
of them, the view that there is no *general* object of
judgment; that all judgments are specific. Only
that thinking is genuine which eventuates in ' judgments of practice.' Now, since we do not act ' in
general,' but always specifically, judgments, too,
must then be specific. On this showing, ' general '
doubt, or doubt about things in general, is not
something to be glorified (as a method or anything
else), but a disease to be treated, like any other
disease, by getting at its cause.

But what if its cause is, or seems to be, the universe? That would bring us back to the ' general ' with a dizzy vengeance. And that is, I believe, just what Holmes would say: that the universe seems to be, and for all we know is, (the object and) the cause of our deepest doubts. Indeed, he almost does say just this in criticizing a remark he had heard that in Russia (old Russia, it was) there were many ' specialists ' in the middle class, but in the upper class there were civilized men. This is his shrewd comment: ' If a man is a specialist, it is most desirable that he should also be civilized; that he should have laid in the outline of the other sciences, as well as the light and shade of his own; that he should be reasonable, and see things in their proportion.' He concluded the comment too long to quote here by saying that the specialist ' should be able not only to explain, but to feel; that the ardors of intellectual pursuit should be relieved by the charms of art, should be succeeded by the joy of life become an end in itself.' Elsewhere he praises the effort ' to see as far as one may the great forces that are behind every detail, and to feel them,' as being ' the difference between philosophy and gossip, between great action and small.' And still again he declares that ' the law will furnish philosophical food to philosophical minds.' So indeed will life, and so everything to Holmes.

Whatever may or may not be true of other prag-

matists, then, we cannot believe that Justice
Holmes substitutes action for thought, in situations that call for thought rather than for action.
Action is sometimes for its own sake, to be sure;
indeed is at its best when it *is* for its sake, as in
play or art. But when it is not for its own sake, it
is for the sake of whatever it is for the sake of.
That is, there are no final and finished criteria.
' An evolutionist will hesitate to affirm universal
validity for his social ideals, or for the principles
which he thinks should be embodied in legislation.
He is content if he can prove them best for here
and now.' But the standards by which men tackle
that job of proving proposed action ' best for here
and now,' or for any foreseeable future, are not
non-existent simply because they are not absolutes.
Indeed, as the foregoing quoted thought continues,
' He may be ready to admit that he knows nothing
about an absolute best in the cosmos, and even
that he knows next to nothing about a permanent
best for men. Still it is true that a body of law is
more rational and more civilized when every rule it
contains is referred articulately and definitely to an
end which it subserves, and when the grounds for
desiring that end are stated or are ready to be
stated in words.'

Rather than saying that Holmes substitutes action for thought, we had best now say that he holds
that no action can be great that is not informed
with thought, redeemed from smallness by perspec-

tive. But no action, on the other hand, can be effective that does not keep its eye on the ball, or, in his figure, on ' the bird.' ' If you want to hit a bird on the wing,' runs his delightful metaphor, ' you must not be thinking about yourself, and, equally, you must not be thinking about your neighbor; you must be living in your eye on that bird. Every achievement is a bird on the wing.' Action, then, is action, and thought is thought; and the twain do constantly meet. Thought, for instance, produces action: ' All thought,' writes the Justice, ' is on its way to action.' ' Every idea tends to become first a catechism and then a code.' But neither the clear articulation of this interrelation of thought and action nor the sharp formulation of the narrow condition of successful action foredooms the Justice to any definition of thought that will tie it down to the ' workable.' There are advantages to philosophy in having its devotee other than a technician, so that he may justly expect to escape the criticisms of technicians and thus be free to say what he means rather than what he can defend against all fencers. Luxuriating in such freedom, the great Justice is not embarrassed by the insight that thought is wonder before it is work, and after work, wonder again. While thought runs naturally to action, it quite as naturally outruns action. We can think, for instance, about the universe, though we cannot do anything about it, save to ourselves as parts of it. And for ourselves, we can do this much at least: accept it, even though we do not and cannot understand it.

This allusion back to Descartes — doing something to himself rather than trying to do something to the universe, you remember, was Descartes' third maxim for safeguarding action from doubt — leads me to suggest, further, that it is in Hume where we find the best clue to this aspect of Justice Holmes. You remember that we discussed and commended the good-natured alternation which Hume practiced with reference to thought and action: thought on the fringes is pleasingly sceptical until you get tired of it; action is thick and joyous at the focus until you've got quite enough. To change from one intolerable to an alternative made delightful by contrast, then when it grows intolerable to change back to the first now tolerable by further contrast — this, we thought, was at least better than bedlam (though to the logical fanatic it would be bedlam). Hume found it more satisfactory than most. There is something of this attitude, it appears, in Justice Holmes. He's clearly all for action. But he's clearly all for thought. He's for each in its place. If they will not stay placed, then let them mix. If you can drive them together — making, as he has it, ' the rule of joy and the law of duty ' one and the same — that's all to the good; if you cannot, leave it to the universe. It tangled things; let it worry about the untangling. Meantime and therefore, every man who has found luck (which, as Holmes says, ' generally comes to patience and talent, if coupled with the love of the thing ') may, with the Judge, ' wreak himself upon life, may drink the bitter cup of heroism, may wear his heart out after the unattainable.'

But there is also the practice more explicitly of another lesson that Hume taught. It is the lesson that, as Hume phrased it, ' we are no sooner acquainted with the impossibility of satisfying any desire than the desire itself vanishes. When we see that we have arrived at the utmost extent of human reason, we sit down contented.' ' Contented ' is a word somewhat too strong to describe Holmes' attitude toward the farthest reaches of human reason, but it is Hume's idea that Holmes practices: what cannot be known need not be known in order to have a good life. Having arrived at the conclusion that, as Holmes says, ' it does not matter what epithets you apply to the whole of things, they are merely judgments of yourself,' Holmes rests in agnosticism regarding ultimate things. I do not mean that he disdains them. He acknowledges that ' there is in all men a demand for the superlative, so much so that the poor devil who has no other way of reaching it, attains it by getting drunk.' Holmes does not disdain it; he forswears it. You'll find few echoes, even in his more free writing, of the sacred verities of many minds no more metaphysical than his own

— God, freedom, immortality. He was relatively insensitive to these even when as youths he and James discussed high things. James once tried to interest him in psychical research. Holmes retorted: 'Why don't you study Mohammedism? Hundreds of millions of men and women think you will be eternally damned without it.' And then followed a conclusion which recurs often in Holmes' later life, being written crucially into one great court decision: 'We go through life staking our salvation on incomplete and imperfect knowledge. Life is like an artichoke; you pull out a leaf, but only the tip is edible.'

More important with Holmes than the humble fact that ' none of us can have as much as we want of all the things we want,' is the intellectual fact that we cannot know all that we want to know. Agnosticism is unconsummated scepticism that has accepted itself for better or for worse. The Justice is simply and finally an agnostic regarding some objects that for some people would be thought to reward chronic scepticism. James, as we have seen, is one of that number, concerned throughout life about freedom of the will, about God, about immortality, and fussing, in his case, for twenty-five years with fakirs, mediums, and saints. It is, no doubt, partly Holmes' wholehearted preoccupation with another specialty, law, which explains his immunity to such things; but, on the other hand, it must not be forgotten that he could have chosen metaphysics rather than law, had he been sufficiently susceptible to that magically retreating boundary that lies beyond and bounds all boundaries. But he was not thus susceptible, and that's that.

But that's not all. Agnostics may be distracted business men, or parochially concentered housewives, or disillusioned theologians, or broken-down metaphysicians, or simple optimists asking for only a little more time. There are many reasons, indeed, why we may sincerely answer that we do not know this or that; we may not care enough to try to know; we may be sufficiently satisfied with other things so as not to think it worth while to know; we may have tried to know and couldn't; we may be pining still to know but just for the moment out of breath. Justice Holmes seems to be an agnostic of still another kind. Neither pining nor repining, neither illusioned nor disillusioned, he has found what it takes to make a life, one life at least, and as for the rest he is content to assume that, apart from an ungrudging acceptance of it, he can serve his old friend, ' the Kosmos,' better by making a life than by out-talking his information about the universe. This trust of the cosmos makes first as a lesson for life what Holmes cites as the first lesson for the student of law, ' that one is safe in trusting to courage and to time.' Meantime, for life if not also for the law, silence remains a virtue.

In the absence of final verity, action does become a great relief; and there is for him, as we have seen, such a thing as ' the joy of life become an end in itself.' He rates very high what he calls ' the pure pleasure of doing the work, irrespective of further aims . . . the triune formula of the joy, the duty, and the end of life.' That's the artist's view. Holmes and James alike, when young, went in for art; both of them forsook art only by carrying her along with them through life. The fact explains not a little about both. Far horizons are but perspective when concern is with the near; but the near is easily enough neglected, in turn, when sunset comes and the eye is gripped by the far, ebbing with and into glory. ' Life,' says Holmes, ' is painting a picture, not doing a sum.' Some action, like a perfect picture, is an end in itself. Some thought transcends action, and ends . . . who knows where it ends? The Truth of all our little truths Holmes is willing to postulate, but he is not willing to be poked about what belongs to his privacy. And such Truth is a faith that's simply and plainly nobody else's business. ' Modesty and reverence,' he holds, ' are no less virtues of freemen than the democratic feeling which will submit neither to arrogance nor to servility.' But our truths, flecked by Truth as hilltops are touched by the sun long lost from view, are everybody's concern. It is a felt disgrace to parade privacy, but it is an open shame not to submit our truths, tested only by agreement at the end of action, to the minds of all, to the acceptance of all, to the correction of all. But this brings us to our final consideration.

V. TOLERANCE OF ACTION AS DOMESTICATION OF STRUGGLE

We have seen the Justice define truth as what he can't help believing. Elsewhere, somewhat more pretentiously, he calls truth 'the system of my (intellectual) limitations.' Now action, when it is not its own reward, aims at fulfilling these limitations. Other men also act, and each actor also has what he ' can't help.' Holmes puts these two insights together in such a way as to get, short of absolute Truth, a developing system of truths; and, short of utopia, a developing society. But both truth and society rest upon very humble foundations. The opening to objective truth he puts in this way: ' what gives it [private truth] objectivity is the fact that I find my fellow man to a greater or less extent (never wholly) subject to the same *Can't Helps.*' The opening to society he puts in this way: ' We have learned to recognize that others will fight and die to make a different world [from the one we are fighting for], with equal sincerity or belief.' In these remarks we have before us the materials for a philosophy of real tolerance.

I say ' real ' for many a man talks of tolerance
without having had it knocked into him by the
rough corners of life, only to have himself fail it
when the crucial test of action comes. Holmes, as
we have seen, had it literally knocked into him in
the stern experience of war. He knows whereof
he talks. Insisting always that others shall ' think
things instead of words,' the Justice gets down to
elementals when he considers man in society. Nor
is the result some glibness about brotherhood, com-
radeship, or Christian charity. He acknowledges
that he has ' no belief in panaceas.' Indeed his
tone is often more akin to hate than to love. And
yet it is not quite either. It is what he calls an
' enlightened scepticism ' producing as its fruits
what we may call an enlightened selfishness (he
himself calls it ' the illusion of self-seeking '). It
is the insight that one himself cannot live and grow
without others about him also living and growing.
But it is a stern thing, never doubt. Against
Kant's glorification of men as always and only
ends, Holmes alludes to our practice of enforced
conscription, he speaks of abolishing the enemy
' not even as a means but as an obstacle; ' and then
he adds: ' I feel not pangs of conscience over
either step.' In a pinch, ' we try to kill the other
man rather than let him have his way.' And the
final verdict of the great Justice upon such treatment of our fellow man is ' that it is perfectly consistent with admitting that, so far as appears, his

grounds are just as good as ours.' Let us get as clear as we can what are the grounds of this hard-boiled tolerance; for otherwise we cannot understand Holmes' work as a judge or extract from his philosophy our final moral for life.

Man does not wish to live alone. Then must he live with others. There is ' no a priori duty to live with others, but simply a statement of what I must do if I wish to remain alive.' Others lay down laws to me as terms of their company, as I lay down laws to them. In so far as these terms laid down by each prove to be common, we have rules of life already accepted by each, though given by all. The situation is, however, both better and worse than that simple statement implies: better in that all of us are more or less pliable and growing and as such now and then glad to accommodate ourselves to novelty, even if it be demands of others upon us; worse in that there is not only an easy limit to that accommodation but also that there is resident in each an indefinite list of intolerables which if others contravene, it is just too bad for them. Holmes does not soft-pedal this hard fact of individual intolerables; rather he erects it into a sort of religion of privacy. ' Our tastes are finalities.' Few idealists but that can and should learn a lesson from this Judge as to the incorrigible conflicts of interests that underlie phrases of cooperation; the vanities of individual phantasy which overlie gestures of charity. He

has not read Hobbes for nothing. Vanity, indeed
— the most ' philosophical' of vices Holmes calls
it — becomes of all vices the one that leans farthest to virtue's side.

And yet cooperation is not impossible. Vanities and privacies allowed for, there remains quite
a large common ground. Vanity itself is no mean
social cement, up to a point. Private vices sometimes become public benefits. There are moments
indeed in which the old warrior almost seems to
think that some substitute might at last become
possible for war as the still necessitated teacher of
tolerance. ' Beyond the vision of battling races
and an impoverished earth' he can now and then
catch ' a dreaming glimpse of peace.' Indeed, he
says, ' if our imagination is strong enough to accept the vision of ourselves as parts inseparable
from the rest, and to extend our final interest beyond the boundary of our skins, it justifies the sac-
rifices even of our lives for ends outside ourselves.' But such perfecting of the imagination as
this can come only by men in general learning far
more than now to respect the privacy of man in
particular and by each man in particular learning
far more than now to keep his urgent oughts to
himself. It is this double drive toward perfection
that the Justice apparently has in mind when he
surmises that most of the things that are remediable have remedy — slow and painful, if possible
at all — only by our becoming ' more civilized.'

If that is too hard for hope, then modest self-understanding as to how one's own preferences came to be final and impetuous, notes Holmes, 'leaves one able to see that others, poor souls, may be equally dogmatic about something else.' This difference runs so deep that on important matters it may be acknowledged that, as Holmes acknowledges with reference to a certain point of law, 'to those who agree with me I am uttering commonplaces and to those who disagree I am ignoring the necessary foundations of thought.'

Now the first thing to be emphasized about such hardy tolerance as this putting up with men who insist on being reasonable or good in such cussed queer ways, as we well know all good men do, is that, learned in action by Holmes, it is applied by him to action. We must, if we are civilized, not only allow others *to be* different and *to think* differently; we must allow them to *act* differently. True, they must not act too damn differently; if so we'll kill them, with a good conscience, or, less heroically but hardly less effectively, we'll 'cut' them with a smile or a shrug. But, intolerables apart, our claim to be civilized must meet generously a wide variety of action. Hear his words upon this point: 'As twenty men of genius, looking out of the same window, will paint twenty canvases, each different from all the rest, and every one correct, so am I apt to think men may be al-

lowed the defects of their qualities if they have
the qualities of their defects.'

The second thing to be emphasized about this
tolerance is that it spells out the formal charter
for democracy. The formal democratic demand is
for majority rule. ' Our test of truth,' he adds as
the permanent value of his earlier bravado definition of truth, ' is a reference to either a present or
an imagined future majority in favor of our view.'
Now from one who finds nothing finally sacred
about even an individual life, you will certainly not
expect to find anything sacred about a majority.

> The huddled warmth of crowds
> Begets and fosters hate.

Nothing sacred about majorities, no. But there is
something singularly convenient about a majority.
And it will be well remembered that Justice
Holmes finds convenience next to godliness,
roughly identifying the law therewith.

Now the first convenience of the majority is that
it is powerful; and even if we sharply distinguish
might and right, as we have seen the Justice does
not, nothing so adds to the dignity of right as
power enough to make itself triumphant. ' If the
welfare of the living majority is paramount,' he
admits, ' it can only be on the ground that the
majority have the power in their hands.' Nor is
it any small moral advantage for a majority that
more life gets lived thus. ' I know of no true

measure of men,' says the Justice, ' except the total of human energy they embody.' And again, from him, the only question as to whether life is worth living ' is whether you have enough of it.' A majority is just plainly *more* life than any minority. But the third and greatest convenience is that any other principle than majority rule is decidedly more *in*convenient. No realist will ever forget that fact; it is the bottom fact. For in a world where perfection beckons but never awaits our arrival, the nearest approach to it is to get as far as may be away from imperfection. Since the Justice suspects all legislation always to be for one class at the expense of another, let us have at least the majority on top; in that way the number underneath is less.

Tolerance, beginning then as personal allowance, ends as the defender of majority rule. Justice Holmes has devoted his judicial life to that defense. That the majority is suppressive, he learned more indelibly from life than from his friend John Stuart Mill. But so is the minority; so is man. There is certainly elemental pity in having suppression, since it must come, thwart more lives than it fulfils. The only way to avoid this elemental wrong is to maintain the majority principle. And the only way to maintain that is antecedently to maintain the forms of consent whereby majorities peacefully become majorities — and cease to be such.

As a judge, Holmes has devoted himself unswervingly to the defense of this double maintenance. He cautions judges themselves ' to leave
room for much that we hold dear to be done away
with short of revolution by the orderly change of
law.' As regards freedom of speech, that major
means of growing majorities peacefully, he has
said: ' We should be eternally vigilant against attempts to check the expression of opinion that we
loathe and believe fraught with death.' And in a
more recent decision he declares that it is ' the
function of speech to free men from the bondage of
irrational fears ' and then concludes that the all
but unexceptionable remedy for excesses of speech
' is more speech, not enforced silence.' Any denial of this is a desertion of the faith of the Fathers,
the faith that ' liberty . . . is the secret of happiness, and courage . . . the secret of liberty.'
Not the dead, however, but the living is his chief
concern. ' The present,' he has ringingly declared,
' has a right to govern itself so far as it can.'

As regards freedom of contract, another means
of consent, he has maintained protection up to the
point that formal freedom to contract endangered
the welfare of the majority. At that point the
safeguards meant by the Fourteenth Amendment
for an oppressed minority he has refused to have
turned against the will of the living majority. For,
in his view, ' the Fourteenth Amendment does not
enact Mr. Herbert Spencer's Social Statics.' The

rights of the living majority has been indeed the polestar upon which Holmes as judicial guardian of democracy has unswervingly fixed his eye.

He has not been stayed from the defense of the majority principle by his own private prejudices. ' I strongly believe,' he acknowledges, ' that my agreement or disagreement has nothing to do with the right of a majority to embody their opinions in law.' He has not been stayed from defending free speech as the major form of freedom by his notions of public fitness. Not even notions that he loathes and believes fraught with death are to be checked, ' unless,' as he now adds, ' they so imminently threaten immediate interference with the lawful and pressing purposes of the law that an immediate check is required to save the country.' Such strong words in the exception strengthen the rule almost to an absolute principle. He has not been stayed from his defense by even his devotion to the truth; for it itself is the test of truth. ' When men have realized,' he says, ' that time has upset many fighting faiths, they may come to believe even *more than they believe in the foundations of their own conduct* [my italics] that the ultimate good desired is better reached by free trade in ideas — that the best test of truth is the power of thought to get itself accepted in the competition of the market, and that truth is the only ground upon which their wishes safely can be carried out.' That, at any rate, he holds to be ' the theory of our

Constitution.' We now know it to be the foundation of his own life.

VI. THE MORAL OF TOLERANCE FROM THE LIFE OF HOLMES

We have seen a tolerance developed by Holmes
in action, for action, put to action in his own official duties. It is something to endure what we do
not like, swallowing our personal disgusts. It is
something more to stomach for the sake of larger
principle what we believe dangerous to the perpe-
trators and to the public good. But it is the supreme measure of stamina to transmute our precious private truths through the crucible of our
disgusts into truths made large enough to house
both our disgusts and the objects thereof. It is an
achievement of this order, if not this very achievement itself, that the life of Justice Holmes exemplifies.

The moral is that a genuine democracy,
whether it be a pearl or not, is possible only at a
great price. Is it a price too great for most men
to pay? The result is that what passes for democracy, where anything still passes, is but the camou-
flaged dominance of an astute minority, or it is
the open and pathetic reduction of men by natural
catastrophe or way to such privation as compels
toleration for some brief spell. But the maintenance by this modern Stoic of the form of democ-

racy when he well knows how morally ambiguous is the matter covered by the form, entitles him, through suffering, to point us the way to the fuller goal, a democracy of matter as well as of form.

The first price which he would ask us to pay for this fuller goal is the maintenance in oneself of an aristocracy of merit. It has often been said that exponents of democracy are aristocrats. This is true in a deeper sense than merely that it is only those who have achieved some distinction above their fellows who can effectively articulate popular rights. It is true also in the sense that men who have found something precious about life as it flickers in the depth of their own souls, think the rights of life in general deserving of defense. Democracy not only assumes potential greatness of soul in most if not all men; it also demands actual greatness of soul in some to voice the potentialities of others and to provide for the actualization of those latent powers. Holmes is preeminently such a democrat. If the democratic form prevails or survives — it can in the nature of the case hardly permanently perish — Holmes is one of its immortals. His doctrines have maintained its form; his life has illustrated its matter.

> When flocks are folded warm,
> And herds to shelter run,
> He sails above the storm,
> He stares into the sun.

There is another price paid by Holmes — I do not say that it must be paid by all. For him scepticism was early mellowed by suffering and subsequently controlled in action. Action, as what he calls ' the mode in which the inevitable comes to pass,' has been kept from dissipation by this sense of the cosmos, which though unknowable is not uninfluential. As often as he voices his contentment at being a part of the universe while he plays the part of a man, he implies this sense of the whole which redeems from insignificance the part played. ' If we think of our existence,' he cautions, ' not as that of a little god outside, but as that of a ganglion within, we have the infinite behind us. It gives us our only but our adequate significance.'

It appears to be this which prevents him from pinning, as he says, ' my dreams for the future to my country or even to my race.' It prevents his usurping the role of deity by out-talking his moral knowledge and suppressing as eternally wrong what he only knows that he does not like. And, best of all, it so enriches his privacy that he actually prefers to live his own life rather than to busy himself keeping other people from living theirs.

> He keeps above the clouds,
> His cliff inviolate.

To an imagination thus enriched ' the forlorn hopes on which we throw ourselves away ' become self-justifying ends. These ends as little lights

for our small darkness he sets, in a famous remi-
niscence of Pennsylvania Avenue by night, in ' a
universe not measured by our fears, a universe that
has thought and more than thought inside of it,
and as I gazed,' the cadence of memory concludes,
' after the sunset and above the electric lights there
shone the stars.'

CHAPTER VII

THE UPSHOT OF SCEPTICISM

Being a moral drawn from morals

Fresh from the invigorating presence of men who have incorporated doubt into their ways of life, we may now say regarding scepticism (1) that it is inevitable for a growing mind, (2) that it can be turned to creative ends, and (3) that it yields the kindly fruits of tolerance to those who are exercised thereby.

I. DEATH THE ONLY ESCAPE FROM DOUBT

That it is inevitable for one growing to doubt, we know from the very nature of intellectual growth. We would not like to be thought a disciple of either Hegel or Marx, but what they agreed upon (considering their deadly differences) might well reward our inspection. Their deepest agreement was that reality moves, whether in the mind or out of the mind, by a process which in the mind at least is the very essence of scepticism. Hegel put the matter in a pompous, Marx in a bellicose, manner. But from the manner of each we can extract their matter for our own ends. They agreed upon a sacred trinity (though one member of it in typical Marxian fashion is quite like the devil) of ' thesis, antithesis, and synthesis ' to mark successive stages of growth. Whether this is the way in which the cosmos ambles along or society moves ahead, we, who like Justice Holmes are not wise to the ways of totality, simply do not know. But that it is the way the mind grows from more to more is certainly not far from the truth. We affirm, we deny, we discriminate — that is the law of living thought.

Take liberty as a good, and study the human approach to it. In adolescence we affirm that freedom is doing as we please; then tiring of that uncharted course we cry, like Wordsworth, for discipline and affirm that true freedom is doing what is commanded (by leaders, principles, or gods); then at last, in maturity, we know that freedom is neither the easy doing of what we please nor the simple surrender to what others please, but the difficult achievement of composing discrepant claims into some sort of moving equilibrium. Liberty as license passes into liberty as discipline to emerge in the well matured man as liberty under law. We have affirmed, we have denied, we have at last discriminated.

That course is but the blue-print we have seen effective in great lives. Descartes, for instance, starts with tradition, passes into general denial, affirms at last tradition as modified by continuing scrutiny. Spinoza starts with both God and the world, loses both, and at last in Substance recovers both in one. Schopenhauer, for instance, starts with suffering, passes through contemplation of suicide as its cure, and ends with an affirmation of Nirvana as the maintenance of Being divested of personality which grounds suffering and which suicide would not effectively purge. Holmes begins by affirming self against the world, then through the discipline of war discovers an order that makes itself effective against the self, and ends by devoting his life to a social order that, under the acknowledged cosmos, composes the conflicts of men through a wise tolerance. It is Montague, however, whom it seems wisest to emphasize as an illustration. He has most thoroughly insinuated the method effective everywhere in science to those subjects that traditionally are thought of in connection with doubt, that is, to such subjects as deity and immortality. To this aspect, with Montague as our example, we shall return in Section II of this chapter. For the moment, however, we must further emphasize not the fertility, but the inevitability of doubt.

If doubt is, as I have been suggesting, the very law of mental growth, then death is the only way to escape doubt. It *is* the very law of growth, for by doubt we do not mean indifference, or laziness, or posing; we mean the active but confused passing from what we do not know but want to know, to knowing it, or knowing that we do not know it, or even that we cannot know it. This is no begging of the question by definition, for the definition is of a process open to observation. The process is that of growth in knowledge. You may take the growth or leave it. If you take it, you'll take it through the avenue of doubt. If you leave it, you'll pay for so doing with death.

This is a bold word, this word ' death.' There are many kinds of death, as there are also degrees of being dead. But a mind that has ceased to learn is either dead or dying. Now no mind renounces all growth along all fronts all at once; and every mind forecloses some issues all the time, and all issues but one, some of the time, in order to focus upon and adjudicate that one. But foreclosure is not the real test of being mentally alive; the real test is the willingness to re-open it upon the presentation of new evidence. As Charles Peirce, the eminent mathematician and philosopher, said, ' the scientific spirit requires a man to be at all times ready to dump his whole cartload of beliefs the moment experience is against them. The desire to learn forbids him to be perfectly cocksure that he knows already.' The ' open mind,' then, does not mean a mind wide open, but one willing and ready to re-open upon demand. That kind of mind is compatible with the preoccupation required by action; and that kind of mind is alone compatible with intellectual growth and integrity.

Men can live, and live nobly, without this or that religious belief, without this or that moral conviction. But they cannot live nobly without integrity. And they cannot have integrity while refusing to face new evidence or while fooling themselves about the old. Scepticism is catharsis for self-fooling, as it is insurance against the risks of premature mental death. Like all things precious, as Spinoza has taught us, it is difficult and dangerous. But for the good life it is indispensable. We may indeed say with Bailey's *Festus,*

> Who never doubted, never half believed.
> Where doubt there truth is — 'tis her shadow.

The world may flee from doubt in fear; but the world will come back to the method of doubt in sanity. Otherwise is all lost; for without integrity all is lost. Capacity, therefore, to stand, and willingness to indulge, doubt are the lasting tests of such a mind. All this we mean when we affirm that doubt is inevitable for mental life and intellectual integrity.

All this we mean and more. The ' more ' is the implementation of this doctrine, negatively, against the easy calls to mental death and, positively, toward the great things awaiting creation through ' modest doubt,' which in Shakespeare's further phrase, ' is called the beacon of the wise.' The latter positive emphasis we defer for the time being, in order here and now to post warnings over the main doors to mental death. Beyond these doors are the Illusion of the Blood, leading downward, the Illusion of Simplicity, leading backward, the Illusion of Certainty, leading inward. But they are all easy escapes luring toward intellectual death.

1. The Illusion of the Blood. Scientific intelligence throughout the civilized world is painfully shocked today by the downward call to men to ' think with their blood.' Tired of being bewildered and rebellious against the slow methods of political compromise, men have in certain crucial segments of life renounced thought altogether. The blood simply does not think, it only feels. To parody Emerson's noble lines to duty is not half so shocking to taste as is this barbarism to conscience.

> So nigh to gory is our lust,
> So near is brute to man, —
> Heart pumps forth a bloody ' Must! '
> Then Duty yields, ' I can! '

To feel is to act, and to act in the name of blood is to act against somebody, anybody; whoever happens to be at hand will do. The fact that in Germany the action falls heaviest upon those who were among the first to introduce, as religious claim, the notion of a superior blood, a Chosen People, does but add to tragedy an ironic note. It does not lessen the tragedy, either of the innocent who suffer or of the guilty who betray integrity to passion. This Illusion of the Blood is, of course, not restricted to Germany. Without it, or its near equivalent, there would be left little heat of nationalism anywhere, and nationalism is the religion of the moment. Italy has listened to the Call of the Blood, and is following its Pied Piper to some sanguine Perfection — who knows where? Japan has long listened to the Call of the Blood, and now is willing to advertise its Illusion to the world as its national mission.

And who are we Americans to boast? The nation as a whole remains still sane at this moment of writing, but a nation whose parts can so easily combine against its parts has no guarantee against succumbing to the Illusion of the Blood. No insurance save eternal vigilance. The threatened revival of the Ku Klux Klan under the guise of saving the Constitution is not the last threat from those who in the name of superior blood will combine ruthlessly against whoever happens to be handy. Modern Paul Reveres, grown pudgy with time and prosperity, may hear the Call of the Blood and ride to the death, rather than to the rebirth, of a nation.

Blood is no substitute for brains, unless Illusion be thorough enough to reconcile us to barbarism. To hearken to the Blood may free from doubt, but it does not insure against disaster.

2. The Illusion of Simplicity. The Call of the Simple is a more appealing escape for some than the call of the Blood. The intolerant thin-blooded will flee to the simple as avidly as the blood-clotted rush to the fray. And where are they to find the solvent simple? In the past preferably, anywhere in the past. In politics, they will flee to laissez faire, leaving most men as hindmost for the devil. In religion, depending upon the prevailing climate of opinion, they will return to Luther, to Paul, or Peter by way of Rome, or in a pinch even to Jesus. In ethics, they will flee to the respectable virtues, and hold sacred as right only the thin glitter time has added to the results of previous might. In education, they will return to the classics, ever and anon to the classics.

The beauty of returning to the past is not that the past is simple, but that some men are. The simple-minded can make the past simple by neglecting of it what they do not want to see. The present has a pestiferous way of refusing to be neglected, though it can be temporarily avoided the ostrich way. But the past is more responsive to wishful thinking. Blessed be the past! What hope is there, however, that a simplicity achieved by easy selection from the past can help meet the present? If it were not for the complexity of the present, which baffles us, we would not flee to the past for its simplicity. What hope is there, then, I repeat, that the fictitious simplicity of the past achieved by selection from the real past will not leave us as impotent when we bring it back to deal with the complex present as we were before we fled from complexity to past simplicity? We have only made our plight more desperate by adding painful illusion to practical impotence.

Let us single out, for illustration, the lure of the classics in education. The notion is widespread and is gaining ground that our present bewilderment can be lessened if not resolved by a return to Thomas Aquinas or even to Aristotle. This retreat differs from the older defense of the classics. Differs at least in being easier. Older American humanists, like Paul Shorey and Paul Elmer More, wanted a return not only to classic ideas, but a return through classic instruments. Having paid the price of mastering the Greek (and the Latin) language, they wanted all other aspirants to get discipline and inspiration the way they got theirs. They followed the lure of simplicity, to be sure, but were willing to pay for salvation by very hard work. The great advantage of their emphasis was that the linguistic mastery which they prescribed as means to salvation resulted in such dependable habits of work and such intellectual discipline in contact with exacting teachers that their educational theory could easily be successful, for a reason wholly different from the one they gave. There was bound to be some fine psychic increment from that type of emphasis upon the classics.

But the current emphasis in education is not so strenuous. It is made not infrequently by young men in a hurry, who would not deign to prescribe such pains, even if they have endured them themselves. Young but tired literary men who seek surcease from passion turn to authoritative religion, and able but impetuous educators turn to classics ' in translation,' to rejuvenate the human spirit. The contrast intended is primarily between hard work which does bring a great reward, nilly if not willy, and a short-cut which seldom is rewarding; a contrast, in short, between devotion to the classics and a dabbling with them. One need not believe in either, but one must respect the older humanism. It was, of course, an escape; but a flight made upon the wings of reality cannot wholly escape reality, however remote may be its destination. But a flight from reality upon the wings of irreality has little to be said for it save that it is Illusion.

We have spoken a word for a genuine humanism without losing sight of the illusory nature of any return to the classics as a way out of our bewilderment. The complex discipline achieved in studying the classics rather than any solvent ideas grasped from them is surely the right point to emphasize. In the first place, modern life has all the classic ideas in its own texture. Plato and Aristotle, Aquinas and Spinoza have entered into the stream of our life and thought. But, says the objector, their clear ideas get so confused in our context that we must return to them themselves to get their ideas straight and clear once more. Now it takes only a school boy to see that the very reason that renders them confused in the modern stream will render them irrelevant to that confused stream once we go back and get them clear at their source. It is the logic of events that troubles us here; we are faced with a predicament, not a make-believe. We need men, not play boys, to deal with our modern situation.

Simple ideas of simpler times (neither as simple as they are made out to be by those who want to believe) are too simple to become solvent ideas for our complexity. That's the reason they lose their clarity in our bewildered world. Not until we face the elements of our bewilderment and elaborate from them ideas adequate to express all elements and direct them together to some end indicated by the nature of the complexity, can we solve our problems. The return to the classic texts is thus seen to be a return to a Simplicity that is too simple for the job at hand. Why, we'd as well propose to substitute mediaeval or classic science. But that proposal is ridiculous upon the face of it — as ridiculous as is the other when you look behind it.

I do not discount the contribution to us of the classics, nor of the Simplicity of their ideas. In knowledge to many but in devotion to none, do I yield in the case of Plato. I read and re-read him for profit as well as for pleasure. But pleasure and profit that accrue in the privacy of imagination may be all but useless for reducing contemporary bewilderment in action. Much as I prize Plato and the keen joy I get from the gems I find in him, I should be hard put to think of a single problem of my own perplexities which he has helped me to solve. The same I have already acknowledged of Spinoza (Chapter III). Their contributions are of a different order. The emphasis upon the classics is but a flight to the past for what will be ineffective in and for the present. It may and will edify the imagination, but if taken for more than that it fools the man. And salvation from contemporary bewilderment must be made of sterner stuff than self-fooling.

3. The Illusion of Certainty. Closely connected with this search in some ancient classics for Simplicity is the Illusion of Certainty in every present. Ideas which the past has chiseled down to utter simplicity do, as we read them, seem more certain than most things of the jumbled present. Doomed by time to death, they rise, in the charity with which we enshroud the dead, as immortally clean and beautifully clear. Others find where they do find, what I acknowledge I find in Plato. But try to utilize their cleanness and their clarity for resolving the modern situation to which they seem most appropriate, and you will have had, or will have, an experience that may well make you ask for a change of venue from the chronological to a logical jurisdiction. That is the distinction which I intend between the Illusion of Simplicity and the Illusion of Certainty.

For the good in the past is presumably not good because it is past; it is good because it is good. That being so, one who acknowledges that the present is the child of the past and that therefore whatever content of the classics that is relevant for the present is enmeshed in its web, such an one need only keep clairvoyant of the vast web around him to have suggested to his sensitive mind what if he got it from the classics would not drip so profusely of the stuff of life. Now a dead and partly dried idea is surely no better for that reason than a live one still juicy with experience. But perhaps there is a compromise between these. Why not isolate by sustained introspection just those elements of our minds, themselves children of the present and grandchildren of the past, which are the solvent connectives in our own loose-jointed bewilderment? Why not indeed?

That was just the tack, as we noted in Chapters II and III, which Descartes, Spinoza, and other early moderns followed in supplanting their doubt with certainty. Simplicity, in other words, becomes a test for certainty, as in Plato's argument on the soul it became a guarantee of immortality.

What is simple in the sense of not being complex,
Plato argued, cannot be dissipated because there
are no elements to separate. What is simple in
thought, so argued the early moderns, is indubitable, because there's nothing about it to distract
attention, and so in it no chance of error. The
phrase ordinarily used by Descartes and his succes-
sors was, however, not ' simplicity,' but the double
description of ' clear and distinct ' ideas. Simple
ideas are indubitable, but by clearness and distinctness shall we know simplicity.

The course of modern philosophy has not run
smooth in this heroic quest. Descartes, let it be
remembered, admitted that there might be difficulty in identifying just the ideas that are clear
and distinct. There was. There was so much
difficulty, in fact, that contemporary moderns have
all but renounced the quest by that chart. We
have heard that matured incarnation of the modern spirit, Justice Holmes, declare that certainty is
generally illusory. And that disclaimer even in
law where certainty ought to be found if anywhere,
and used! Montague, systematically and honestly
facing the situation, has, as we noted, renounced
certainty in favor of probabilism. Another great
modern whom we have not mentioned as yet, John
Dewey, has also renounced certainty; has renounced it and published his reasons in the book,
The Quest for Certainty. Now one would think
that, in the light of all this, before thoughtful men

became discouraged enough with moderns to flee them for mediaevals or ancients, they would modestly inquire whether the trouble may not be with the situation, with the world, rather than with the modern temper and its representatives. Where men with such acumen as have the moderns and such aid, of both instruments and history, find so little of certainty, there may actually be no more to find anywhere than they have found.

But are there not simply some truths self-evidently so? Justice Holmes has enabled us to make severely simple our answer to this recurring question. Nothing is self-evident except what is so; and nothing is to be counted as so upon which intelligent men disagree. Agreement of the competent, then, becomes the only scrupulous test of what is actually and publicly self-evident. Certitude is easy for any ignorant or biased mind, the more ignorant or biased the easier; but certainty which self-evidence means to declare, that's harder. We need others to make sure of most things. To rule others out of the class of the competent because they do not agree is not only unscrupulous but also asinine; for it leaves colossal egotism alone in step. Now any interpretation by the competent as to what is so, will not only disclose few things as self-evident, but will disclose the further fact that the claim of self-evidence is in discussion a technique for squelching dissent rather than for declaring or getting agreement.

It is not a technique for declaring agreement, because it is ordinarily made only when disagreement has persisted until all other arguments have been exhausted. It was so in the Declaration of Independence, as we remarked in Chapter I; it is so in the latest scrap between labor and capital. It is not a technique for getting agreement, for the claim is in its essence an assault if not an insult. No disputant has ever been convinced of a point by another's declaration of its self-evidence. In argument we want evidence that this or that is so, not evidence that somebody feels that it is so, even though he may feel it very strongly. Let him keep his feelings to himself and show us the evidence. The truth is that to declare self-evident what another person is arguing against is to make, if not to call, either him or yourself a fool. Though the calling is meant for him, the making is clearly enough for you. Only a fool would declare certain and settled what is still being argued; only a fool or an infallible one. And whoever in such a situation thinks himself infallible *is* a fool. No, an argument has little weight with the other fellow when the major premise of it is that he is a fool; he's seldom fool enough not to see through and to resent that trick.

Then do I mean to deny that 2 plus 2 make 4 for certain? No. I have not denied that some statements are true. You may even call them self-evident if you wish, but you will please confine that term severely to what we agree upon, unless you wish me to call you another. Without going into the question as to what makes such a statement seem so certain for both of us, I agree that 2 plus 2 are 4 for certain. And there are other statements also true for certain. But they are all of a type. I do not say that they are not important, but I do say that all of them bound together and used as a ramming rod would not make a dent on contemporary bewilderment. Our bewilderment is of action rather than of pure thought. If we knew what to do, we would be little worried as to what to think. And learning what to think by looking backward or inward or upward is not going to show us what to do in our complex situation. I do not deny that any one of these may make us happier if we do not have to act; they may even make us better. But they will not make us less bewildered when confronted with action in a situation that simply outruns our knowledge. Indeed, to get a beautiful self-evident truth as key to a bewilderingly rusty lock and then find that it simply will not fit, is an experience none too rare but one which only adds worry to bewilderment.

Justice Holmes is not only modern but also wise in declaring, as we have seen, that no concrete proposition is self-evident. I have spoken above of all self-evident statements being of a type. One aspect of the type is that it is abstract. Kant was clear that abstractions without concrete contents are empty. But Kant was another modern! Well, Plato wasn't a modern, though he too, like many moderns, lacked a classical education. He was nevertheless wise enough, in an ancient sort of way, to acknowledge that his prized abstractions, the Ideas, would not in themselves facilitate action, not even the simple action, as he puts it in the *Philebus,* of finding one's way home.

Would not ' in themselves,' I say, facilitate action? There is, it is true, involved in all intelligent action, as well as in all thought, an abstract element; and this abstract element may well partake of the nature of certainty. But this admission affects in no way the previous simple contention that not all such certainties put together can render completely certain the simplest action, however rationalized the action may be. This view we have already developed in connection with Spinoza. Of angels this or that may be true, or nothing, for aught I know. But of men and their action, I affirm uncertainty for certain. All that I am here interested in establishing, however, is that an appeal to the self-evident in situations calling for the empirical, reflects upon the intelligence of the one who so appeals. It does nothing to others save to inspire them with pity, if they are philosophic; with anger, if they are not.

Self-evidence, then, is no escape from bewilderment whether derived from the Illusion of the Blood, of Simplicity, or of Certainty; for what is

246

certain is so because of the absence of the elements which make for bewilderment. When the elements are present, bewilderment results and remains, spite of flight backward or inward or upward, until we face the situation itself and distill from it such assurance as probability makes possible in dealing with the empirical. ' For better or worse,' says Montague, ' life is utterly committed to going forward. It is too late to retreat.'

II. Doubt Can Create Compensation for Uncertainty

Now this is the place where the lives of men who really have achieved something can help us. We return to our heroes after finishing with the legions of death. It is of course in modern science where the intellectual and the practical meet most fruitfully.

And who is better prepared to guide us here than the great Pasteur? He it was at the dedication in Paris of the Institute that bears his name who warned fellow seekers for truth as to the danger of prematurity in the pursuit of knowledge. ' This that I ask of you,' he said simply, ' is what you again in your turn demand of the disciples who gather round you; and for the investigator it is the hardest ordeal he can be asked to face — to believe that he has discovered a great scientific truth, to be possessed with a feverish desire to make it known, and yet to impose silence on himself for days, for weeks, sometimes for years, whilst striving to destroy those very conclusions, and only permitting himself to proclaim his discovery when all the adverse hypotheses have been exhausted.'

' Yes,' continued he with a brevity almost poignant, ' that is a difficult task. But when, after many trials, you have at length succeeded in dissipating every doubt, the human soul experiences one of the greatest joys of which it is capable.'

As against the little men who rush into action against whomever at the call of their blood or other little men who rush into abstract thought for a shot of sustaining certainty to nerve them for action before something spoils, here in Pasteur a great scientist speaks, bodying forth the calm and poise of science itself. He had known what hard days and sleepless nights meant in plowing through doubt toward, ever toward, truth. What little truth there is for men is, he knew, too precious to be thrown away for a mess of impetuosity. No chance could be taken either with the truth or with the integrity of the seeker. Hurry might spoil both by premature claims. Such was his private code. Such the code enjoined upon fellow workers. Pasteur was a great scientist.

This code enjoined by Pasteur is to an astonishing extent the code prevailing in contemporary science. The very enterprise itself lifts many little

men into devotion to a greater than they, devotion
to a cause that achieves dignity by claiming to be
the custodian of truth. There is something highly
inspiring in this devotion, and something deeply
reassuring in its caution as the major means of our
own method of doubt. The contribution of that
method through science is doubly great. The
labor lifted off the backs of men through scientific
inventions marks man's promotion from the animal to the human level. Retarded mastery of social means necessary for the full appropriation of
the fruits of science need not obscure from us what
those fruits are. Leisure is available for the good
life whenever we learn how to appropriate these
fruits. And they are concrete and substantial
fruits of scepticism, for without this element of
doubt there would simply be no science at all.
Pious tradition had long ago closed too many doors
to the seeker, marking them, as Huxley said, with
the sign, ' No Thoroughfare! By order of Moses! '
There are many types of markers, in many names
besides Moses; but science just goes doubting
along without seeing any of them.

Greater, however, than its emancipation of men
from dogma, greater than its practical effects which
spell abundance rather than scarcity — greater than
these is that other fruit of science to which Pasteur
refers in his address. Success ' in dissipating every
doubt,' gives ' the human soul one of the greatest
joys of which it is capable.' No lover of knowl-

edge can doubt that. Truth applied to life may indeed make men free, but apart from any application the discovery of it can for a fact give the thrill of a lifetime. Spinoza has taught us to think of it as blessedness. What comes to the scientist, who at Pasteur's price of pain transforms private certitude into such certainty as men call truth, is debased by comparison with the cheaper joy of one who impetuously calls his certitude certainty without having rendered it so.

Now, difficult as has been and is the maintenance of the tentative mind in science, it is more difficult in common life and even in the segments of philosophy which we have mostly attended to in this book. Science has after all a tradition of tentativeness, sanctions of ostracism for such scientists as violate the tradition — sanctions that are ruthlessly enforced, too, by that hard-boiled community — and rewards of pride and place commensurate with the pains involved for those who pay the price of doubt and finally win through to truth. Common life, on the other hand, sets everywhere the tradition of jumping at conclusions, of believing what you want to believe, and of distrusting if not actually punishing the men of the open mind.

Remember, in America, the obloquy heaped on Ingersoll, whose chief offense was that he insisted that ' an honest god is the noblest work of man.' Remember the fictitious death-bed scenes fabricated to terrify the unrepentant and then fastened on David Hume, on Thomas Paine, on Voltaire, on anybody reputed to be an unbeliever, by those falsetto voices of commonsense, the itinerant preachers of American protestantism. Recall the shudder along the whole respectable front of contemporary commonsense at the mention of Clarence Darrow, a man willing to suffer for his belief in humanity but a man who also, alas for respectability, publicly purports to doubt the efficacy of vindictive punishment and who wishes he could, but honestly cannot, believe in God and immortality. How many of these and those humbler unsung atheists of every village besides, have not cried out with Thomas Hardy:

> Yet I would bear my shortcomings
>   With meet tranquillity,
> But for the charge that blessed things
>   I'd liefer not have be.
> O, doth a bird deprived of wings
>   Go earth-bound wilfully?

While commonsense has been and is far away from the fruitful tentativeness of science, and from the toleration of those who are not so far away, philosophy is nearer but not much nearer. The greatest tradition in philosophy since Socrates has been to find good reasons for believing what you already believed without any reasons. It marks some advance indeed on the long road to truth to insist on any reasons, even if they be

' good ' rather than ' real.' But it marks a further advance, an advance by leaps and bounds, to that shining goal when a philosopher, like Montague, combines the common man's will to believe no matter what, with the scientist's will to doubt until you are entitled to believe. In Montague, as we have seen, we have a sort of combined Pasteur and St. Paul, willing ardently to believe, like a Paul, but willing even more ardently to believe only the truth, like a Pasteur.

Even more important than either the will to believe or the will to doubt, is the will to estimate probabilities, i.e., to believe by such degrees as the growth of evidence justifies. This is the scientific spirit at last illustrated in religious and moral fields. It is much easier to deny outright, even with a shrug, what common men believe, especially when you are not much interested anyhow in the matters at hand. I do not doubt that some of the disdain men have felt for religious doubters and moral iconoclasts has been invited by the manner of the dissenters, and even some of it justified by an inordinate degree of negation. It is difficult if not impossible for a genuinely scientific mind, for example, to get beyond honest agnosticism to dogmatic atheism in religion. And men have reasons for expecting dissent from ethical standards and denials of humane hopes, like that of immortality, to be moderate in statement and constructive of intent. Not only is such an attitude more scientific, it is also more educative. Heavier dents are made in our own armour of dogma by diplomacy than by the big guns of counter dogma. Pending education through open avenues of communication, the dissenter asks only tolerance, and giving this is more effective for getting it than is his asking.

William James was the first great scientific mind in America, I believe, to illustrate the high virtue here recommended. He preached the ' will to believe ' but he practiced as have few ardent souls in fields of hope the ' will to doubt,' pursuing psychical research, for instance, for a quarter of a century with hope undimmed but judging still open-mindedly at the end: ' Evidence as yet insufficient.' His practice of the strenuous virtue lent the weight of sincerity to his preaching of the humane vice. His sympathy for the pathetic need on the part of men to believe, opened an avenue for his personal caution to penetrate and do its judicious work. George Santayana's genial gibe is almost the literal truth about William James: ' He did not really believe; he merely believed in the right of believing that you might be right if you believed.'

In this hopeful spirit of openmindedness James was the forerunner, as he was the teacher, of Montague. When the limitations imposed by James upon the will to believe are emphasized, as we have no occasion here to do in detail, his doctrine is little different from that of Montague. But Montague, as the James of this generation, has stated the moral very simply and quite fully. James opened a crack for the scientific wedge by practicing an austere virtue while indulging a popular vice. Montague is driving that wedge deep into the common mind of our time. He is, as was James, a happy go-between of science and commonsense: he has all the enthusiasm, the drive, the yearning, the positive-mindedness of the common man; and he lacks little of the scepticism, the caution, the trustee-mindedness for truth of the scientist. The result is what we have seen in Chapter V.

In his philosophy we have an avowal of belief rather than of knowledge. We have precious questions of freedom, of immortality, of divinity lifted from the slough of feigned indifference or of smart negation to the plane of ardent hope and tempered expectation. But the hope is held in leash by defining the expectation as being precisely what it is: the estimation of probabilities that already exist and the increase, in whatever way is open to us, of those probabilities. Meantime, intellectual integrity is preserved by a clear distinction between certainty and probability, and sanity is maintained by a clear recognition of degrees of belief. Such a temper and approach promises the maximum of direct fruits from doubt in the moral and religious field, but it also promises no less of the indirect fruits of good will and mutual forbearance among men. This, however, is our final topic. To it we pass at once.

III. TOLERANCE AND THE DEMOCRATIC WAY OF LIFE

It is the supreme virtue of tolerance that constitutes our final moral. Justice Holmes has hitherto been our guide and exemplar in this sector of our quest. Learning the lesson, as he did, in war, he struck us as hard-boiled. Two lessons we glean from him, however, as we could not from any source less austere. The first is that social hope does well if it builds a tolerable society on earth, forgetting alike the heavenly hope of early Christianity and the classless dream for the indefinite future of contemporary communism. Fixation upon perfection foredooms to frustration. Overdevotion to the very best retards the achievement of a better which might otherwise be. A touch of realism is a necessity for any effective idealism. The second lesson from Holmes is that what as strictly private may be beautiful to the point of finality easily becomes when publicly exhibited an offense to taste and an enemy of dynamic order. This insight we illustrated in Chapter VI, in connection with Holmes' reverence for the cosmos. I hope my readers sensed through the lines quoted from the Justice what I felt deeply as I read him, the pathos of his acceptance of the universe. A successful struggle with emotion is, as every actor knows, a more effective means of communicating it than is overt expression of the emotion. The great actor's lips only quiver where the amateur would break down and cry.

Furthering that vulgar figure, Holmes never breaks down and cries. His hopes are his and private; they move us because they are so. His fears are his and private; they touch us to the quick because they are so. He not only proclaims the sacredness of privacy; he practices it as a judge, by protecting the majority's conscience and freedom of experimentation from that powerful minority, the Supreme Court; and then in turn by staying the hand of that majority itself when it is uplifted against a private individual's right to think for himself and even to express those thoughts. As a man he practices the virtue of tolerance by refusing to let his taste and even his private convictions of right and wrong rule him as judge, as well as by maintaining his individual right to privacy against the world.

This distinction between what is privately permissible and publicly impermissible is the thought which draws together the beginning and the end of this book and justifiably conscripts lives of certain great men to exemplify the unity. This is a distinction we all acknowledge when we see it merely as a matter of taste, but which few acknowledge when it appears a matter of morals or of public policy. We acknowledge that men may differ in tastes; we often even welcome such differences as adding variety to life and lustre to association. We do not acknowledge the same of moral, and not always of religious, convictions. Might not the tolerance of tastes be indefinitely extended in the field of morals?

One hundred years have, of course, marked a tremendous extension of tolerance in the religious field; three hundred years make all the difference here, from open persecution nearly everywhere to open toleration in not a few nations. The Illusions of both Simplicity and Certainty are now held in check by a tradition of tolerance in the fields of both taste and religion; only nations blinded by the Illusion of the Blood go back down the slowly built steps of tolerance to barbarism at the bottom.

How arduously built were those steps in religion is emphasized by remembering that they had also to be built in humbler matters of taste. Let Kipling summarize in verse what as scientific history we would have to extend too lengthily. Neolithic Man knew how to make short shift with hostile critics:

I stripped them, scalp from skull, and my hunting dogs fed full.
And their teeth I threaded neatly on a thong;
And I wiped my mouth and said, ' It is well that they are dead,
For I know my work is right and theirs was wrong.'

Why not, I repeat, make this already brilliant extension of tolerance more brilliant still by extending it indefinitely to moral and civic convictions? There is only one answer which the open mind can hear; and that is that moral and civic convictions lead to action, and action on the part of some closes doors to others (as well as to the 'some'), doors not closed by thought or even talk. This is a distinction, indeed *the* distinction, which Justice Holmes has drawn. He draws it in such a manner as to make our moral quite manifest: *suppressive action can be justified only by subversive action or by immediate and certain incitement thereto.* Now the temper of Justice Holmes furnishes what these or any words lack. It is the temper of *giving the benefit of the doubt to freedom:* freedom of thought, of speech, of action. The deep human drive is to give the benefit of every doubt to suppression. And there are many places where this narrow edge of interpretation counts as final. There are men, and women too, who need no further proof that the social order is threatened than the fact that their feelings are hurt. Justice Holmes deprecates all projection of such private feelings into public invalidation of freedom. 'I regret,' runs one of his dissenting opinions in behalf of freedom of speech, 'that I cannot put into more impressive words my belief that in their conviction upon this indictment the defendants were deprived of their rights under the Constitution of the United States.'

Now, none can use more impressive words than the Justice, and he did his best in that case. Words are not enough to check suppression, for the intolerant spirit will take from words as from situations the benefit of the doubt. It is safe to say that no large body of men has ever yet consistently acted upon the determination to see how much freedom of action could be allowed to all men without dire ruin resulting. It was once felt that the degree of freedom of thought now encouraged in democratic lands would, if allowed, bring down the heavens upon men. The heavens still stand. Freedom of speech? The degree we enjoy would simply have wrecked, it was thought, any past authoritative order. Democratic social orders certainly stand as secure as others; immeasurably more secure where the practice of freedom has been well matured as a tradition. There may well be room short of ruination for more variety in action than even democracies have dreamed of practicing. John Stuart Mill grew desperately afraid of the coercive threat of the majority; but it will be time to worry deeply about that when the danger is less pressing of the same, but worse, coercive action from minorities.

The truth is that it is hardly time to talk of any extension of the principle of freedom into further action when the freedom already won — of thought and speech — is in jeopardy, wherever not already in ruins. Spinoza, the world hath need of thy voice in this cause! In a world where liberal action is forfeit to necessity, liberal thought must voice itself the more. Such thought sees clearly that suppressive action has falsely anticipated dangers not inherent in freedom. It has struck at its own ugly shadow, and has blindly struck down it knows not what. But we know what it has struck down; it has struck freedom down; and freedom's death makes a spiritual desert of all lands where it lies buried. Oases in which freedom still thrives can be for the liberal spirit but outposts from which to plan reclamation of desert lands from drought.

The strategy of the re-conquest, however, cannot in most cases use the weapon made odious by the enemy, suppression. Intolerance lies back of suppression, and intolerance is not cured by suppression. The bald truth seems to be that often it is not cured by anything. Where cure is out of question, it may yet be checked by force. No liberal in this unsteady time dare be any longer squeamish as to the use of the last resort against intolerance which boasts that once it has the power it will repay indulgence of itself with prison or death. All virtue is departed from a virtue used to abolish itself. *Tolerance for all the tolerant; and intolerance only in defense of tolerance.* But

at that last ditch let every cohort of liberalism kill
to live or die in honor of the right to live free,
rather than live in the dishonor of having betrayed
freedom through a qualm. The hardness of the
old soldier, Justice Holmes, is needed to nerve
liberalism at this crossroad of modern life, nerve it
to do or to die.

But this strenuous mood and attitude will ordinarily be overtly necessary against only those
whose will to suppress springs from the Illusion
of the Blood. The other Illusions that we have
noted can still often be reasoned with, though it
will pay one to keep his hand on the trigger, in a
spirit of hopeful fear, while reasoning with some
of their devotees. Tolerance *from* them is the
end of the tolerance *shown* them; and prudence as
to when to expect what, is a high virtue of war. It,
no doubt, taxes one's ingenuity, even if his patience
is adequate, to deal further with one who, suffering from the Illusion of Simplicity, adduces his side
of an argument as being veritably the idea so clear
and distinct as to validate itself, like some local
ontological argument. And it is no easier to know
how fruitfully to proceed in association with one
who, suffering from the Illusion of Certainty, settles
the point in dispute by declaring it self-evident.
One can remind both these, however, of Lincoln's
story, which ought to be on the fly-leaf of every
logical primer in the world. It is so simple that
even a fanatic could read it on the run. Lincoln

declared, you remember, that to call a mule's tail a leg does not make five legs, but only four legs and one liar. If a joke whose moral is fairly pointed does not penetrate, then one might appeal to the delicacy which sometimes renders even egotism fastidious.

For there is something unseemly about the public parade of a private feeling of certitude as objective certainty. One must be allowed to feel that things are true; he must be even allowed to feel that they are self-evident; but in the presence of equally intelligent persons who deny them, how can he be allowed to claim them self-evident for more than himself? For him to do it is equivalent to his calling a fellow man a liar. That is indelicate when done in good temper; and it is an insult when done otherwise. If a reminder of delicacy does not suffice, then must we lump the devotees of Simplicity and Certainty with those fanatics of the Blood, and gird ourselves for war — war to the hilt and to the limit. Liberalism can tolerate such intolerance only while it is weak and still may respond to the therapy of modesty.

All of which is to say that while the feeling of certitude is a precious thing when treated as a private possession, it is only a rude will to power when it seeks to extend itself to others. We must recognize every exhibit of self-evidence as an indelicate baring of the private, or as an intention to dominate others. The counterpart of each of

262

our three Illusions, when insight is insisted upon short of a general agreement of the competent, is intellectual dictatorship. Only an authoritative institution, like the Catholic Church, can resolve the difficulties spoken of by Descartes as limiting the utility of clearness and distinctness as criteria. Without such backing to resolve difficulties that just will arise with even Simplicity itself, the claim is no good; and with such backing it is no good to a free spirit, who does not wish intellectual matters settled for him. Only an intellectual buccaneer will resort to self-evidence as criterion of certainty, and such an one is out for power not for truth.

But we close in mood more affirmative. We plunged you into scepticism at the beginning for a wholly constructive purpose — to make you tolerant. We have wanted only to show you that, however much you think you know, you simply do not know enough to justify intolerance on grounds any higher than hate. ' No man so sure as Omar once was sure.' There may be some whom, as Dante says, ' doubting charms not less than knowledge.' But we are not of that school, nor have we — save for Pyrrho — exhibited men of that way of thought. Taking doubt as inevitable for an honest mind intent upon growth, we have learned where we could, even from Othello,

263

To be once in doubt
Is once to be resolv'd.

We have paraded only men as heroes who could
say with Stanislaus, once King of Poland, ' To
believe with certainty we must begin with doubting.' We have not been minded, as saints of old,
to believe the ridiculous in order to know the holy,
but we have sought, with modern saints of science,
to fructify our necessary doubts with such knowledge as the universe allows to intelligence.

Truth is a word of many meanings. But if we
approach it in the mood just indicated, we may
say that truth appears to be primarily of two sorts.
There is the ' true for me ' and the ' true for me
and others.' There may be a third kind, ' truth
itself.' But since we can never know it directly,
the matter really boils down to holding the ' true
for me ' or the ' true for me and others ' as *the*
truth. Now the final determining factor in the
choice between these options, as in every important
choice, is a moral one. Only the egoist will identify *the* truth with the truth for him. The very
fact that one does so is itself warning enough to
others that his action will be of a piece with his
logic. The identification of *the* truth with the
' truth for me and others,' spells tentativeness regarding anything that so far is true merely for me.
Science in exemplifying this virtue becomes the
custodian of morality in the intellectual field.

Science is thus related to democracy in ways more deep than mere production and spread of concrete goods. It is spiritually related. Its tentativeness of temper makes for tolerance in the social field. If you cannot make men cooperative through wisdom, you may be able to keep them tolerant by convicting them of ignorance. Scepticism offers ends of great joy, the discovery of truth; but it constitutes a means of very great moderation in the practice of dominance. Nobody does in fact know enough not to welcome the cooperation of others in his quest for truth; and those who think they do, know less than most. To bring home to men how little they know for certain is to rob intolerance of its last garb of respectability. Scepticism is not only the great antiseptic for the wounds of the spirit; it is the only known guarantor of modesty enough to make society possible without constant suppression.

Gladly to let live is the only way to live greatly. Whoever has doubted through to this truth, has beaten himself a path to civilization.

DATE DUE